MW00931354

THE
OMEGA SHIELD

Sequel to "Navigators on the Edge of Forever"

BY D.M. YOURTEE

NETWORK IS FORMING
OMEGA IS APPROACHING
IS THERE A SHIELD?

THE OMEGA SHIELD~~

THE OMEGA SHIELD
Future Navigator Armor
A Minds-Eye™Book*, Copyright © 2017, by D.M. Yourtee

All Rights Reserved. No part of this book may be reproduced or transmitted in any form by any means, electronic or mechanical including photocopying, recording or by any information storage and retrieval system without permission in writing from the author.

This book completes the account in 978-0-692-77138-9 (Future Navigators on the Edge of Forever, 2016). It includes condensed and updated subject matter from ISBN: 978-0-996-88239-2 (The Future Navigator, 2015) by D.M. Yourtee.

The editorial opinions in this book are those of the author or persons he or they met or as described and attributed in the text. Any resemblance to any other persons, living or dead is purely coincidental. This work employs some philosophical language. Sincere effort has been made to couch the language in normal text terminology, to provide definitions, and to credit authors who might have contributed first time postulations.

An original prequel is available through the Library of Congress via reference Publisher's Cataloging-in-Publication Data, "Journey into the Light" / by D.M. Yourtee.
   p. cm.
   ISBN: 978-0-615-58784-4
   1. Spiritual life—Fiction. 2. India—Fiction. 3. Africa—Fiction.
   PS3625.O99   J68   2012
   813—dc22   2012900393
To order books see http://www.aminds-eyejourney.net or write Minds-Eye@bresnan.net.

Published by Minds-Eye Manuscripts, LLC
Grand Junction, Colorado, 81505

Great minds must be
ready not only to earn
opportunities
but to make them work
for everyone
with
the real end in mind!

EX LIBRIS_____

PROVISO and DEDICATION

This book is about reaching into the deep future. So it does involve a need to address new terms. The reader thus made aware, can if preferred first use the glossary (p.144) and then turn to the story.

The story is built upon the remarkable insight of a handful of visionary thinkers who lived in the times of awesome discovery, the times of Einstein's proposals and of the beginning of much of the incredible communication devices developed for today's world.

These thinkers proposed the futuristic agenda that allows us to focus on the most important challenges leading to a successful outcome for human kind.

The work is therefore dedicated to them - whose names will unfold as the story is progressing.

~~~~~~~~~~~~~~~~~~~~

The Empires of the Future
Must Become the Empires Of The Mind!
From
Winston Leonard Spencer-Churchill

FORWARD

Most of us experience but do not really "see" the dominant influence of world-wide-communication. Of course, our communicating to each other-interlinking the globe began sometime back. But, now its vastness, its deep influence on our minds is growing day by day, indeed minute by minute!

This leads to the proposal, quite realistic, that we humans if not now, will soon be functioning under one network, a Global Brain! Thus, as a species we will be heading somewhere gradually growing better or worse toward a fully unified cyberspace existence. Our world will then be reaching toward a "Vistavia" a final "Homo definitivien" existence one which some scholars have chosen to call Omega, i.e. the "Omega Point". Their vision sees that as an awesome, beautiful out bursting into eternity!

In the story to follow the realistic expectations and needed solutions address Omega with hope of developing a shield for everyone so that eternity will, indeed, be reached in safety and wonder.

Human Kind has a destiny in Forever, which we cannot fully envision. It could be tragic or with hope truly magnificent. That destiny, however, no matter how we may see it in our personal beliefs is now controlled by the ever increasing massiveness of cyberspace. What is it that may shield within that influence-our humanity and take us along safely with the developing Global Brain, such that our final destiny is indeed Stellar?

REACHING FOR OMEGA

CHAPTER 1: THE "FOREVER PANEL" CONTINUES

(Leading to a MostThoughtful New Focus!)

The boat cruised in, incredible powerful sounds clapping the waves as it headed straight toward the sand beach between two islands near the southern tip of Somalia.

They were waiting there almost in awe as the MkVIPB the Navy's next generation Patrol Boat (a part of the Navy's Expeditionary Combat Command's fleet) came toward them. The mission was appropriate although this rescue was on the edge of the usual!

The MkVI Patrol Boat provides operational commanders capability to patrol shallow areas beyond sheltered harbors and bays, and into less sheltered open water for the purpose of protection of friendly and coalition forces and critical infrastructure. The Patrol Boats two powerful diesel engines mated to water-jet drives allowed the joystick controlled patrol boat to hit speeds over 35 knots as it headed in. The site is awesome, she is bristling with weaponry, including a pair of remotely operated and stabilized 25mm chain guns and six crewed 50 caliber machine guns in her configuration. All this, however, mattered little for the current job!

Three, haggard, turbaned figures were waiting there, one with white skin, he hobbling aid of a cane. This was many months after he was thought to be burned to death in the crash of a disappearing commercial air-liner!

Later, rescued onto that PT boat, remarkably back at home he called a get together of his special research group!

The man with the cane was Dr. Daniel Jordyn. The Doctor's Laboratory was on the frontier working to develop living cells to replace those needed in injury and other very difficult healing circumstances. This was not an economic pursuit or for him a drive to the Nobel Prize. His personal mission was to help extend life aiding humanity itself into the distant future! Daniel was as we see not a timid thinker. That is, he was skirting the very wild idea of creating ever-lasting life!

His research group shared his vision and the mission. They considered themselves "Future Navigators". And, incredulous as it seems they had been on retreat in India sharing with others an inquiry into what really is "Forever"! They were attempting to clarify the related idea, one most everyone believes exists, i.e. if there is a Forever. What really is it? And although (again) that seems rather absurd, the aim was to determine accessibility, i.e. a view into the Future, by inquiring into the governing principles of Space-Time.

This pursuit was not an amateur exercise. It was through an academic meeting of experts called "The Forever Panel". Nonetheless, how near insane that appears, at least they learned from their inquiries that "Forever", is indeed! And, specifically it is an "Infinite Physical-Chemical Mobius Reality". That is one, fixed and working in ways that knowing the future is way beyond our current ability.

Suffice it to say, having returned home, the Doctor called a meeting of his "Research Family". From this group there were ten members all once in the Future Panel as following.

1. The Professor himself is Daniel Jordyn. Name Italian sounding, as often pronounced Jordin-e' but descent is Germanic. "Dr.Why" as he is fondly known is Full Professor of Medicine, with specialty in Biomaterials as replacements

for injuries to extend life. He is experienced in world travel, an American Fulbright Scholar involved in humanitarian research in Africa. He is a widely published scientist but also the author of eight books in the area of "Objective Humanism" a conduct of life philosophy, which champions preserving through tolerance the distant future for the world's children. He was raised Methodist but has over the years become more Pantheist.

2. Dr. Samyak (Darshon) Jain. The last name is indeed Jain as is carried by all so born. Samyak's name means philosopher-visionary fitting his life's accomplishments. He is a retired professor of World History and greatly respected for his wisdom and insight, justly known and honored as a Magi. Jainism has some similarity to the broader belief in Hinduism which he practices as totally nonviolent and benevolent. He together with his daughter Daya served as hosts for the meetings of the Panel when in India. For the lab he is an ongoing consultant. Samyak and his daughter Daya were brought to the U.S. on a visit after the panels retreat in India, and a personal connection was also at hand as Daya is mother of one of the Panels sons.

3. Professor Ahab Singh. He is Middle Eastern Indian. However, he is of mixed ethnicity and is proudly Muslim. Dr. Singh is Full Professor of Astrophysics, Delhi University. He is a-political, devoted singularly to the pursuit of clarity regarding space-time a subject that Professor Jordyn recognizes the Panel will need to have as consultant for many of their projects. Dr. Singh is one of the many arising advocates devoted to understanding quantum mechanics as it relates to the infinite Universe.

4. Dr. Timothy J. Bean. Dr. Bean, holds a Ph.D. in Biochemistry with emphasis in Biophysics. He is a post-

doctoral student in Dr. Jordyn's Laboratory in charge of their cell i.e. Biomaterials Project, that is, synthetic cells being created to help fight severe injuries (they are referred to as the BIOS+). He is a devout environmentalist and frequently joins in the gatherings of these groups who are objecting to all the thoughtless environmental damage, and believes in the threat of global warming. Tim's father is English. His mother is from Bosnia and was an expatriated Jew. Although he was raised Jewish, his father is Christian - Church of England, and so he considers himself "Seeking". He has returned from India after a Post-Doctoral there at the Patel Institute.

5. Dr. Pi Su chien Hsu. Dr. Hsu holds dual Ph.D.'s In Physics and Mathematics. She has taken the anglicized version of her name as Pillory (Pi for short). Her doctorates concerned challenges to the Einstein's supposition of the constant speed of light in time's conjunction with space. Pi is the nick name she genuinely accepts it being of course the same as that famous one for the product of the ratio of the circumference of a circle divided by the diameter. Pi's family are followers of Confucius, though Pi holds no faith or dogmatic philosophy. She is rather certainly atheist and committed to seeking astrophysical undersanding of life. Just as Dr. Bean she is returning to the lab after a Post-Doctoral at the Patel Institute.

6. Master Chief, James V. Skellan. James is nicknamed the Hawk, because of a face injury suffered in his Navy Service as an EOD or explosive demolition expert. The Hawk is retired Navy Master Chief, with extensive experience disarming explosive devices almost everywhere in the world. He has made it his personal mission as he traveled to learn about the world's faiths, their successes and failures. Both he and the Professor have been schooled in the

50 "Principles for Centering the Mind", a fundamental schooling for persons who are devoting their lives to Future Navigation, i.e. as the Professor he is committed to doing what he can in his area of expertise to insuring the survival of the world's future children. Skellan is a prized member of the group because of his extraordinary clear thinking (a certain necessity of the job as EOD and his centered clear mind).

7. Chandler Nowell Caldwell, M.S. Chandler is an Architectural Technologist holding an M.S degree in Mechanical Engineering. His wife is Jane Caldwell, the Technical Recorder in the Professors Laboratory. He joins the panel through deep interest in the future although he holds a critical ability as one who understands issues concerning structure and is also an expert in computing, internet, electrical conductivity and related.

8. Dr. Jehan Nirupuma. Dr. "Jehan' is a Professor of Medicine, who is responsible for "Life Perspective" teaching in her University. She is Pakistani by birth, but was raised in India as an orphan stemming from a terrorist attack during her student days. Dr. Jehan did a search in Africa for the "Teacher of Tolerance", where she was once again under terrorist threat as prisoner in a Wahhabi Enclave. She is Hindu. She wrote a document in defense of children the "Declaration of Light"…and receiving the teachings of the visionary See-ela (called a "Vistavien") has in turn taught those to the Professor and Skellan, i.e. Dr. Jehan is a pivotal educator in "Future Navigation" for all the group.

9. Jane L. Caldwell, M.S. Jane is the technical recorder for the group, the one who has written this "Panel Profile". She is also ongoing secretary in the Professors laboratory. Jane is mother of three who are now in teen-age, a catholic in

faith. She holds the M.S in forensic science, though she truly loves her recorder role in the laboratory.

10. Angelei Skellan. Angelei following her husband Skellan travels became an expert, the most informed of all in panel on faiths and philosophies around the world. She is of such depth in the subject that she consults for the group on all matters pertaining to faith or philosophy needing unbiased input.

This panel to a member felt that it was time for someone to really look into that age old idea that we each have a "Forever" and more they are united in discovering ways to insure that there will be a future for all.

Being called together once again by Dr.Why was most precious as these all had become not just co-workers but emotionally much a family!

So the meeting, the reunion called by Dr.Why was to take place and it was as always when in the U.S. In the "old digs", that is, the back room of the "Newport" a most popular bar (and Grill).

When Daniel came in, leaning heavily on his cane, they all stood up cheering and applauding having lived through a time when they believed he had died in that crash. So-to at first avoid putting him on the spot, possibly making him uncomfortable each member of the group told of their own stories when returning to the U.S.

For most it was the usual, long crammed in–flights, working through customs and in the case of most as Jane, spouse Chandler and Jehan warm return to families.

Doctors Tim and Pi were in Delhi for Post Docs at Patel Institute, so were not able to return for several months. Pi. told a troubling account because she was assumed from her oriental appearance, one to be ultra-questioned and was held for a while, under a tighter (and new) immigration protocol. Her trip in rerouting, led her to a stop in northern Africa and some very uncomfortable nights in what was basically a ghetto hotel. She in fact was accosted near a store an event that did not last long as Pi as in everything she does had mastered Taekwondo. Shortly after she was able to return, there appeared on the streets three Arabic men with considerable face bruising!

Tim made it back all the way home but had the unshakable memory of his grandfather's grave being vandalized with Nazi Swastika when he took his Jewish mother to the cemetery for her monthly respects. That as it seemed was happening around the country, a largess many assumed to be a creeping standard in his beloved U.S. (where the just elected President seemed to forget he was a mixed people's servant, and the internet abounded with bigotry).

These tragedies born by the two were held even more in mind as they were also, in their life's' work goals---looking toward ways to reach the long term future for mankind. They knew more so than most, understanding forever, that it means whatever we make of ourselves, we will be forever for everyone. The center of attention of that trip back though was to be focused on the Professor's tale of his remarkable return.

"Well it is all due to Skellan and a kindly Arab", he said as he started out. "And, if my old friend hadn't stepped in for the rescue, I wouldn't be here. The crash was in southern Libya and all were killed except me and a lovely young woman, the two of us laying there amongst the horror of burning and bodies. She managed to pull me free, and we lay in a ravine for at least two days, no one coming, the plane not located."

THE OMEGA SHIELD~~

"Finally, a group of Arabs, found us and we were hauled off to a hut, belonging to an eastern Libya tribal group. The young woman, most tragically passed about a week later her injuries must have been deeply internal. The people we wound up with were thankfully peaceful, though they might have held us thinking of the potential for ransom. I believe these were "Bani Zoghba" who originally, after settling in Tripolitania and Gabes, were expelled by Banu Salim to the eastern parts of Algeria, and currently they are found between Bjaya and Telmsan (place easily found on the maps, but then unknown to me). In the end though, these people couldn't decide what to do with me!

Turned out that they brought along with me what I was wearing, the belt was still there with my little pouch and miraculously my cell phone, and some little battery still there worked just enough to give approximate coordinates to Skellan.

Don't know much of the rest of the stay in Libya, spending time in and out of consciousness. But Skellan somehow reached out to someone he knew there from his EOD bomb-diffusing Navy time and I found myself on a truck full of food stores, rice they were calling Bariis, traveling further through Libya, then across Ethiopia heading deeper south east and winding up near Hudur, a military complex located in southwestern Somalia. There in a rather happenstance village I was put in the care of a non-Somali ethnic minority group made up primarily of the Bravanese, Bantus and Bajuni. The Bantus are the largest ethnic minority group in Somalia. They are the descendants of slaves who were brought in from southeastern Africa by Arab and Somali traders.

Well, I won't go on and on about that except to say, they spoke Swahili so most fortunately my Fulbright experience came into play and I was very lucky indeed. I think these folk were thinking about ransoming me! However, one of them had a terrible sore running down his back into his rear. I had of all things some lip balm, and a piece of candy with cinnamon. With some water and then some of the local peanut oil I made a creamy slave, knowing the cinnamon would be anti-infective (crossing my fingers). The long and short of it was (probably crazy luck) after about a week the man's sore cleared up and I won a deep new friend! This man was then able to take me to the Hudur base where I contacted Skellan again. He would be unable to pick me up in Hudur, but a pick up from the Bajuni Islands[1] off the coast of Somalia would be possible, as the Navy was patrolling that area in hopes of holding off Somali Pirates.

The Hudur coordinate, I will never forget them is sitting at 4°7'12"N 43°53'16"E. These were corrected to a pick up site just on the coast of one of the islands where the pickup could occur. Then it was that I was able to have my new friend struggle me there, various transport, and await a boat. This all must have been a trip of a couple thousand miles, so

1. The Bajuni Islands, also known as the Bajun Islands or Baajun Islands are an archipelago in the Indian Ocean, situated on the southern coast of Somalia, from Kismayo to Ras Kiyamboni. They lie at the northern end of a string of reefs that continues south to Zanzibar and Pemba. It is of note that the president's travel ban meant, Sudan, Somalia and Libya remain banned, for people to enter the U.S. from there. Navy ships fitted with heavy weapons are reported to have arrived in the Somalia territorial waters and set up base around Bajuni Islands of Kudai, Ndoa, Chuvaye, Koyama, Fuma Iyu na Tini and Nchoni Islands, during the Islamist insurgency of 2000 and fortunately for the Professor, they still held presence there as the Somali Pirate scourge continued.

I am so very thankful for that Arab (name Absamea) who supported me the journey. When I was in Africa earlier in my life I learned quickly how most people have an inborn sense of humanity, which of course holds for many although surrounded by horrible poverty and killing!

Even so, I have to tell you all it was one of the highlights of my life when we saw that boat swing around the reef and head straight to us. I knew Patrol Boats as a sailor-corpsman years back when in the Navy, but when the sound of those engines on that awesome modern version, the Mk VI PB resounded in our ears, my eyes just dripped tears of joy.

The boat of course took me to a U.S. Hospital Ship harboring near Australia, some healing and ultimately home to you all, and that my friends is all thanks to Skellan and a very noble Arab man!

The doctor hobbled over to where that old sailor was sitting, hugging him as the whole group cheered and applauded so loud the Newport bartender opened the door and gave the please quite sound.

The meeting that then proceed was to say the least deeply welcoming and warm, all sharing their most recent experiences.

Jane and Chandler had us laughing at the funny things the kids did. Jehan shared her experience with the new rather green med students, and Pi and Tim shared the news of their forthcoming marriage...the ceremony, they said would be one to attend, a cross between the traditional Jewish and some oriental admix.

There had to be, of course, this first discussion of all that is happening around them, and what occurred to get back. However, this group live and breathe proposal, questioning, and intellectual pursuit!

So it was very soon that things turned academic as one might suspect from such and egg-headed clan. It was at this first meeting that they decided to continue their "Future Navigator" gatherings and continue meeting at the Newport Bar, the place where their Forever Panel was conceived and that pursuit now was published[1].

So, as though it was born in inertia, the subject turned immediately to their shared objective the long term future of humanity, which they know (now) cannot be predicted, but there is deep concern. They know humans are special, unique as they may be alone in understanding the secrets of life.

Dr. Bean said, framing the question for the whole group, "Dr. Why is right---we have an embedded sense of empathy, a sense of humanity. We know Forever will not let us see into it, that is what will happen in the coming millennia." But how much of that can be understood and they worried about that, as it is indeed, in their fiber. Jane said, OK we can't predict tomorrow, but perhaps we can imagine what can be done to insure the best long outcome!

Chandler looking around the room, pausing then asked. "Ok, but do they, these Homo sapiens, deserve such consideration. I mean are we really unique?"

So first is that question of uniqueness, which was addressed by Jehan, who certainly knew of human potential!

"Understanding Forever, we know that its chemistry will explode again and again, unknown number of big bangs, so what is our importance, our likely uniqueness? If you permit let me review for us briefly, and I mean rationally."

---

1. The beginnings and further history of the "Forever Panel" can be found in the book "Future Navigators on the Edge of Forever" ISBN: 978-0-692-77138-9 (2016).

And she gave a bit of a review as follows. "The Fermi paradox or Fermi's paradox, named after physicist Vicente Fermi is the apparent contradiction between the lack of evidence and high probability estimates, e.g., those given by the Drake equation, for the existence of extraterrestrial civilizations. The basic points of the argument, made by physicists Vicente Fermi (1901–1954) and Michael H. Hart (born 1932), are as follows.

There are billions of stars in the galaxy that are similar to the Sun, many of which are billions of years older than Earth.

With high probability, some of these stars will have Earth-like planets (as astronomers are currently seeking, some discovering) and if the Earth is typical, some might develop intelligent life. Indeed, some of these civilizations might develop interstellar travel, which is as we know a step our Earth's scientists are investigating now.

Even at the slow pace of currently envisioned interstellar travel, our Milky Way Galaxy could be completely traversed in a few million years, a short span in space-time.

According to this line of reasoning, th*e Earth should have already been visited by extraterrestrial aliens*!

In an informal conversation, Fermi noted no convincing evidence of this, leading him to ask, "Where is everybody?" There have been many attempts to explain the Fermi paradox, primarily either suggesting that intelligent extraterrestrial life is extremely rare or proposing reasons that such civilizations have not contacted or visited Earth.

In short we are unique creatures-at least, and with our abilities deserve to last, but with inability to see into the future, how do we do that, what influences us most?"

Tim, very excited about the question, puts in a worthwhile comment. "I will stand on my comment about uniqueness and it is more. *Our success so far has been due to our sense of benevolence-our humanity.* If not that we would not have survived. Just think of that, over history, time and time again, against the scourges of cruelty, from the Nazis and on and on, that has kept us going. And we are now trying to see the goodness of our democratic ways against the ongoing Religio-polimics, the "Spirit Wars" as Dr.Why calls them." *So to get into the far future, we must understand our direction better, what else has and will influence us?*

Well our history is a kind of covering that is influencing our future evolution. In short and in a nutshell, in the main and to focus...*What we are talking about, i.e. all that matters as to our ability to deal with the future is the question of the greatest influence on our EVOLVING HUMANITY!*

OK, then that is right, subject is "Evolution" Pi set in, "what was, what is and from that what is likely to be. Perhaps what counts here, first is what we know here on earth actually came about, us eventually being a part of that!"

And Tim was quick to seize on that..."So, let me set a kind of backdrop. Having my Post Doc experience on biogenetics, I should spend a moment on our own earth history its "Biogeochemistry" and its relation to us from that! What do you think? I mean, hey you all, really, I won't make this technical...just an overview."

The Professor seeing, perhaps a too technical "deflection" but also sensing agreement from the group on the subject of "Future Evolution" indicted..."Good idea Tim! That could clearly lead us to an important understanding. What is human influence on their home, and the converse... it on our future, what could be our own long term existence, all factors, given the various realms into which we humans inquire... if you will." And I think we should look deeper also, for example into what kind of existence we are really experiencing. For example, perhaps we should look at the importance of our communications, its impacts on our past and future, as in our communication to each other--- it has been and will be central to our future, our evolution!"

"So, let me suggest a way of approaching this. Both you and Pi have completed related post-doctorals to cover the necessary basics for us in shall we say three weekly seminars. And, the Doctor then said looking encouragingly his way and pointing at him, "Mr. Vicente Costa our new student (and Lab Tech) could be working toward a dissertation on, well if I may propose a title "Future Human Evolution", Yes!"

"Vicente, to center this, could you consider posturing your dissertation, on that subject we just exposed, i.e. "Communication"! That is, how has past communication between us humans likely effected our future environment and how is our new global communication going to impact the ultimate fate of Humanity! This will fit I think because of your ability to cross the world-shall we say- as you come to us-with a major and masters in computer networking."

Since the mission of the Lab is to find ways to help mankind toward the future, all carrying the flag of "Future Navigators" this laid down very well with everyone in the group and the new Ph.D. student clearly was excited about the possibly of a focus for his dissertation that fit well with his background!

The Professor encouraged Vicente, looking at him directly. "Yes, it could be, that is, it is justifiably a dissertation! I gather that is, indeed, compatible with your background? Certainly the lab would support that. And the faculty are likely available for a committee here at the University-in our history and computer sciences departments.

So, as you focus your research your opinions and findings would define the ultimate subject, which of course you will stand to defend, an experience there you know having done so with your master's thesis.

Vicente now fully synchronizing with the whole idea, said "I will be honored for the opportunity!" (He was told as a boy his name sake was "Vicente" Blasco Ibáñez the highly admired Spanish writer. Consequently, he carried that name identity always within himself feeling he was destined to be a fluid writer and advocate.)

So, the boss said, "let us get this underway. Next week, we will have the first report, a mini-seminar first by Tim, then one by Pi following on Dr. Tim's report. Dr. Pi what do you think?" Pi in her way, of course, had no difficulty, always cutting just the briefest size response simply replied, "My Pleasure! The direction, must of course, lead us into "Long Term Future Human Evolution", that is the subject of central importance if we can presuppose there will be a distant future given all the insane things people with no sense of history get us into!"

So it was the Future's objective for the Panel was re-kindled and after warm good wishes for the evening the members of the team, new ideas exciting their very deeply inquiring minds, left for home.

Regarding that, here is a look into the home life for a sampling of what we now should call the "Future Evolution Panel Members". This look into home life…is observing the Skellans, sons Gabriel and Andrew.

On this evening they have a guest in Vicente, who is temporarily rooming in their home, until he can establish rooms for himself.

Skellan and Anjelei are watching their son Gabriel teaching his younger brother Alexander how to make bread! Alexander it needs be said is just a very little boy. Vicente knows Gabriel as a navy hero and one to be greatly admired. One would assume from his courageous accomplishments that he might be, shall we say "macho", and not really interested in house-hold chores. Vicente is fascinated with the scene though because of its seeming domesticity, far outside of what he would expect from Gabriel, who is in an apron.

Skellan seeing Vicente's curious viewing of the event, comments. "Vicente, believe it or not this is in the way that made Gabriel strong. Of course not just making bread, but learning all the basic skills of survival at a very young age, that is the means to take care of oneself. Before he was nine, he could do great carpentry, had a full garden, and was reading into the classics. We raised him toward having an independent mind, making his own way, free from superstation. That he gained knowing---the "Principles for an Open Mind" as passed on from the original teacher, we in the "Future Navigator Team" knew as "The Vistavien", and to that we used our insight into the ideas in Maslow's "Hierarchy of Needs" a theory in human development and psychology proposed by Abraham Maslow in his 1943 paper "A Theory of Human Motivation". You are welcome to a copy of his book if you like.

Vicente---as he asked "What kind of bread Alex"---responded, "yes, I would love to borrow that book!" (And Alex answered, "It's my version of potato bread, darn good if I do say so myself, I will give you some.")

CHAPTER 2: THE HUMAN OVERSEER'S FATE

So as planned, about five p.m. a week next, in the evening, lab work complete, the panel gathered at their familiar haunt, once again the back room in the Newport Bar (and Grill). After drinks were obtained and each found their favorite place in the room and around the table, Tim got a "Seminar" underway. "Ok, team, let's go! In process I will do a good deal of definition, and use terms some may not be familiar with, but the concepts are really straight forward, really!"

As he began, you could tell Dr. Bean was totally excited and into his topic, this clearly from his "teacher posture". "Biogeochemistry is our first subject, as agreed. This is the scientific discipline that involves studying the chemical, physical, geological, and biological processes and reactions that govern the actual composition of our natural environment here on precious earth!"

"These concepts to be more specific in terminology are the biosphere and the cryosphere, the hydrosphere, the pedosphere, the atmosphere, and the lithosphere.

I am being deliberate, the "sphere" language here is a form of linguistic mimetics but in these cases does amount to real spheres of influence!"

"In particular, biogeochemistry is the study of the cycles of chemical elements, such as carbon and nitrogen, and their interactions with and incorporation into living things transported through earth scale biological systems, of course, in space through time. And that we on the panel understand is a part of an infinity of our physical-chemical Forever."

"The biogeochemical field of study focuses on chemical cycles which are either driven by or influence biological activity on our planet. Specific emphasis is placed on the study of carbon, nitrogen, sulfur, and phosphorus cycles. Biogeochemistry is, thus, a systems science closely related to Systems Ecology. Sorry, definition may help, recall that Ecology is the branch of biology that deals with the *relations* of organisms to one another and to their physical surrounding.

The founder of Biogeochemistry, and from whose work I report was the Ukrainian scientist Vladimir Vernadsky a Russian geochemist, whose 1926 book "The Biosphere" (in the tradition of Mendeleev) formulated a *physics of the earth as a living whole, that is, the earth as a whole living being!*

That I am sure as we go forward must be constantly in mind! *We will need to view our planet and what goes on with it, including us, as an organism, a living whole!*

We now of course, most of us, do appreciate that reality with the onset of global warming." (There was from this informed group a good deal of comment at this point, mostly as to how so may humans ignore this, heads in the sand so to speak.)

Staying on course though, Dr. Bean continues "Vernadsky distinguished three spheres, where a sphere was a concept similar to the concept of a phase-space[1].

He observed that each sphere had its own laws of evolution, and that the higher spheres modified and dominated the lower! They are as follows…

~~~~~~

1. A phase-space is a multidimensional space in which each axis corresponds to one of the coordinates required to specify the state of a physical system, all the coordinates being thus represented so that a point in the space corresponds to a state of the system.

1. The Abiotic sphere - all the "non-living" energy and material processes.

2. The Biosphere - the life processes that live within the abiotic sphere, and...

3. The Nöesis or Nösphere - the sphere of the cognitive process of man! This is one of the results of our existence! That is, human activities (e.g., agriculture and industry) modify the Biosphere and Abiotic sphere."

In the contemporary environment, the amount of influence humans have on the other two spheres is comparable to a geological force! This comprises a new field of insight! "

"Well to continue..The American limnologist and geochemist G. Evelyn Hutchinson is credited with outlining the broad scope and principles of this new field. More recently, the basic elements of the discipline of biogeochemistry were restated and popularized by the British scientist and writer, James Lovelock, under the label of the "Gaia Hypothesis". (Note all, Gaia is via Greek mythology-personification of the earth)."

"Lovelock emphasizes a concept that life processes regulate the Earth through feedback mechanisms to keep it habitable!

Given the importance of the topic, there are biogeochemistry research groups in many universities around the world. Since this is a highly inter-disciplinary field, these are situated in a wide range of host disciplines including: atmospheric sciences, that is, biology, the ecology, geo-microbiology, environmental chemistry, geology, and oceanography and soil science. These are often bracketed at Universities into larger disciplines such as "Earth Science" and "Environmental Science". I think it is a mark of our fundamental humanity, an Engram, if you will, that this caring area of study has found many homes. And, this research has obvious applications in the exploration for ore deposits and oil, and in remediation of environmental pollution!"

" However, that aside…Now, though… the reason for going on about this… a very important aspect on this, which clearly relates to the distant future of humans is something called the "Anthroposphere". Which Pi, I believe is your pursuit, as we agreed, yes!"

Dr.Why, indicated "great introduction Tim, and yes Pi, where are we going from here?"

She began…"Well dear colleagues, following on my assignment and providing the backdrop for Vicente, yes, I will say a bit about the "Anthroposphere".

This in a manner of speaking lays right on top of Tim's "Biogeo" discussion (group chuckles). That is, clearly, a subject of total contribution to our long term future, i.e. we are in effect, that is for simple survival we are by default, and must be more so, the "Overseer's" of our very precious home! There is though, a terminology that applies!

The Anthroposphere (sometimes also referred as the Technosphere) is that part of the environment that is made or modified by humans for use in human activities and human habitats. It is rightly classified, if we think deeply of it, really as one of the Earth's Spheres, that earth a living whole! And Humans in effect are, as said, this Earth's Overseer!

This continues the terminology that Tim relayed…i.e. *"Spheres"*, since they encompass the earth that is a really easy to grasp notion. We encompass the earth's fate that is up to us, how we function in our Anthroposphere.

As human technology becomes more evolved, such as the greater ability of technology to cause deforestation, the impact of human activities on the environment potentially increases. This leads us into a type of anthropogenic metabolism, and its output, the "Novel Ecosystem".

These "Novel Ecosystems" are human-built, modified, or engineered niches of the Anthropocene.

These ecosystems exist in places that have been altered in their structure and function by human agency. Novel Ecosystems are part of the human environment and niche (including urban, suburban, and rural), they lack natural analogs, *and they have extended an influence that has converted more than three-quarters of wild Earth!"*

"A Novel Ecosystem is aptly described as one that has been heavily influenced by humans but is not under human management. A working tree plantation doesn't qualify under this particular terminology. However, one that was abandoned decades ago would."

Well, to further define, the anthropogenic has "Biomes". These include technoecosystems that are fueled by powerful energy sources, fossil and nuclear-including ecosystems populated with technodiversity, such as roads and unique combinations of soils called technosols. Vegetation on old buildings or along field boundary stone walls in old agricultural landscapes are examples of sites where research into novel ecosystem ecology is developing."

"In fact, Human society has transformed the planet to such an extent that we may have ushered in a new epoch that should justifiably carry an expansion of the title I just gave, that is we are in the "Anthropocene Epoch" as coined by

serious scientists. That is certainly a part of "Human Evolution", now and in the future! "

"Again, this is all surrounding our spherical earth, and so justifies labeling the influences we talk about as "Spheres".

And, again, the ecological niche of the anthropocene contains entirely novel ecosystems that include technosols, technodiversity, anthromes, and the something thence aptly called and I am sure will become extraordinarily important in our discussions.. The "Technosphere".

These terms are deliberate as they describe the human ecological phenomena marking this unique turn in the evolution of Earth's history! "

"The total human ecosystem (or Anthrome) describes the relationship of the industrial technosphere to the ecosphere. Let me define them, these terms, briefly.

Technoecosystems interface with natural life-supporting ecosystems in competitive and parasitic ways.

Current urban-industrial society not only impacts natural life-support ecosystems, but also has created entirely new arrangements that we can, indeed, call techno-ecosystems. These new systems involve new, powerful energy sources (fossil and atomic fuels), technology, money, and cities that have little or no parallels in nature. *At the root of both our future survival and our potential demise is the matter of energy source and utilization.*

Yes, even though Novel ecosystems are creating many different kinds of dilemmas for conservation biologists to this we must now consider something called Anthropogenic Biomes i.e. in other terms *"The Total Human Ecosystem".*

The Anthropogenic Biomes tell a completely different story, one of "human systems, with natural ecosystems embedded within them"! This is no minor change in the story we tell our children and each other. Yet it is necessary for sustainable management of the biosphere in the 21st century.

The researcher Ellis identifies twenty-one different kinds of anthropogenic biomes that sort into the following groups: 1) dense settlements, 2) villages, 3) croplands, 4) rangeland, 5) forested, and 6) wildlands.

These anthropogenic biomes (or anthromes for short) create the technosphere that surrounds us and are populated with diverse technologies (or technodiversity for short)."

"And here is a very telling fact…within these anthromes the human species (one species out of billions of earth creatures) appropriates 23.8% of the global net primary production. Hence, there is a vast energy expenditure!

"This is a remarkable impact on the biosphere caused by just one species." And it has arisen through the last several centuries from ever increasing technology, ever increasing interconnection between the people of the earth."

"Here are terms applied to various aspects of the anthropogenic biomes system.

The technosphere is the part of the environment on Earth where technodiversity extends its influence into the biosphere.

Virtually every aspect of analysis into the Anthorpocene biomes reveals an increasing time dependent alteration of the human world."

Thus, for example, Technosols are a new form of soil group in the World Reference Base for Soil Resources (WRB). Technosols are "mainly characterized by anthropogenic parent material of organic and mineral nature and which origin can be either natural or technogenic."

There is precision in terminology needed of course, for the development of suitable restoration strategies."

"Suffice it to say, with most careful analysis, ecologists stipulate that the weight of Earth's technosphere is calculated as 30 trillion tons, a mass greater than 50 kilos for every square meter of the planet's surface."

"Such Technoecosystems interface with and are competitive toward natural systems.

Such is reality, Technodiversity, is creating an ever increasing time accelerating impact on the future of human life here on earth! This is becoming ever more relevant with our power in communicating what we observe so that we can increase or if appropriately carefully reduce the effects!"

Then Pi, looking intensely at her audience says, *"It is all now and will be here and in the future in the hands of our ability to communicate with wisdom!"* After which, she stops and listens because…

…Here Vicente, taking courage in hand before the very learned group, interrupts… "Yes, if I may, I can contribute here a bit, as in my masters I studied something called…The Wayback Machine. The Wayback Machine is giving us awesome insight into whatever we may wish to influence. All information is becoming available to go either way for our future, good or bad."

"The Wayback Machine is a digital archive of the World Wide Web and other information on the Internet created by the "Internet Archive", a nonprofit organization, based in San Francisco, California, United States."

"This Internet Archive launched the Wayback Machine in October 2001. It was set up by Brewster Kahle and Bruce Gilliat, and is maintained with content from Alexa Internet. The service enables users to see archived versions of web pages across time, which the archive calls a "Three Dimensional Index". The Wayback Machine has been continually archiving cached pages of websites onto its large cluster of Linux Operating System Nodes. It revisits sites every few weeks and archives a new version. Sites can also be captured on the fly by visitors who enter the site's URL into a search box. The intent is to capture and archive content that otherwise would be lost whenever a site is changed or closed down."

"The overall vision of the machine's creators is to archive the entire Internet! Thus if you will --- no effect on us will be lost, the preservation of history is there i.e., our global memory, which is so important to preventing mistakes, if interpreted wisely."

"The name Wayback Machine was chosen as a reference to the "WABAC machine" (pronounced way-back), a time-traveling device used by the characters Mr. Peabody and Sherman in The Rocky and Bullwinkle Show, an animated cartoon. In one of the animated cartoon's component segments, "Peabody's Improbable History", the characters routinely used the machine to witness, participate in, and, more often than not, alter famous events in history."

"To show how powerful this machine is already, let me refer to its' computer termination, i.e. as an Internet Archive called "The Petabox".

"Here are a few highlights about the Petabox storage system. There are 1.4 PetaBytes/computer rack that is 100 plus Terabytes/rack, 4 data centers, 550 nodes, and 20,000 spinning. Total used storage, as of time my thesis was written, was--50 PetaBytes! In the development is Tech-Target whose own site offers a useful point of departure for thinking about how big a Petabyte is. "A petabyte is a measure of memory or storage capacity and is 2 to the power of 50 bytes or, in decimals, approximately a thousand terabytes! (The memory in my new laptop is listed as one terabyte.) Currently there are on board this Way-Back millions of books/music/video and various collections: amounting to 9.8 PetaBytes. Contained are unique data of thousands of different kinds and types of information...amounting to 18.5 PetaBytes!"

The successful deployment of this kind of data to list just a few, gives Internet Archive's replication ability for major academic institutions, digital preservationists, government agencies, Major research sites of all kinds to include agronomy, medical imaging providers, digital image repositories, storage outsourcing sites, and many-many other enterprises around the globe".

"And, there is no doubt what-so-ever the PetaBox storage technology is expanding steadily!"

"That must remind us of an awesome power we humans have and what is involved within us.... Does it not? Therein lies a complete record of all that everyone does and most importantly could share, and, there is potential that it is entrench-able into their thoughts."

"It marks a very special interrelation we have with the earth, and ourselves a complete perspective into ourselves and everything in and on our planet.

I know, sometimes I kind of think randomly, but to this comes my recollection of the "Kardashev Scale", which, not incidentally, I researched via the Way-Back Machine!"

"The Kardashev scale is a method of measuring a civilization's level of technological advancement, based on the amount of energy that an advanced civilization is able to use for communication.

The scale originally proposed had three designated categories and people now suggest seven-the later which take us way into what many would consider science fiction.

Nonetheless, I present this as our concern is "Human Evolution Coming", and it relates to that over long terms assuming survival. So here is a sampling of the Kardashev scale (somewhat updated)." Vicente shows preparedness as he hands out the following list which he reads...

"Type 0 civilization – also called planetary civilization – can use and store energy which reaches its planet from the neighboring star.

Type 1: civilization can harness the total energy of its planet's parent star (the most popular hypothetical concept being the Dyson sphere that is a device which would encompass the entire star and transfer its energy to the planet.

Type II civilization can control energy on the scale of its entire host galaxy."

"The scale is of course hypothetical, and regards energy consumption needed on a cosmic scale. Various extensions of the scale have since been proposed, including a wider range of power levels (Types 0, IV and V) and the use of metrics other than pure power!

Nonetheless, this is a reflection on evolution, is cognizant of our intense need for energy to survive and has some worthy considerations in terms of time frames. The expanded set with example (anticipated) time frames is as follows:

Type 0; a civilization that harnesses the energy of its home planet, but not to its full potential just yet. As you might have guessed, that's our present humanity. We're currently, according to some experts are at about 0.73 on the Kardashev

Scale. It is presumed we'll reach the next, i.e. type 1 in about 100 years, plus or minus, depending on how fast our technology advances and how diligently we procreate. Michio Kaku suggests that humans may attain Type I status in 100–200 years, Type II status in a few thousand years, and Type III status in 100,000 to a million years.

Type I: This references a civilization that is capable of harnessing the total energy of its home planet. This is where we're heading, whether we want it or not! Thus, it expresses an aspect of our future evolution. The good part would be that we'd achieve an ultimate peak, the bad part is that we'd then soon have more energy demand than supply, because evolution can't be so easily halted. We would have to leave Earth and start pumping other planets for their worth, or even milk our own star directly for its power. Regardless, becoming a type I civilization is considered by some as an overall a good thing.

As a type I civilization, we would, it is proposed, be capable of controlling Earth entirely, maybe even influence the weather, control volcanic eruptions and earthquakes, influence global flora and fauna, geological makeup, plate tectonics, etc. That seems awesome! But there is a flipside, we'd have to recycle everything to get by! And of course this all depends on how we behave, which must come from inside us, our inner motivations and sympathies, our sense of humanity, caring for others. Present behavior, well--- trouble!

Type II: These people must be an interstellar civilization, capable of harnessing the total energy output of a star. This is the next stage in the evolution of a civilization, and presumes a level of technological development that allows for gigantic constructions and utmost efficiency. Dyson structures would be proposed here, i.e. hypothetical megastructures that completely encompasses a star capturing most or all of its energy, thus power. A type II civilization would not just build these megastructures, but also inhabit them and completely control what goes on inside them. It would control the orbit of all planets in that system, harvest asteroids and comets at its leisure, and basically consume the entire solar system. An intimidating power to behold! Of course, from our current perspective we see such as fictional dreams! But do recall that 100 years ago we would never imagine, Neil Armstrong's appearance on our moon. Well to go on….

Type III: This would necessarily be a galactic civilization, capable of inhabiting and harnessing the energy of an entire galaxy. Here, of course, we start to venture into truly extraordinarily wild science-fiction territory. And, yes, I am smiling at this, but keep in mind we are focusing on the next human Evolution. Thus, a type III civilization would span the entire galaxy, colonizing and controlling numerous systems. It would be able to harness, store and use the energy output of all stars within that galaxy. Such a civilization would use planets just like building blocks, being able to move planets from one solar system to other, merge solar systems, merge stars, absorb supernovae, and even create stars. The galaxy as one writer put it, is their playground, and everything in it becomes a toy!"

I have read the account of Forever composed by the folks of this lab, and your premise that it is an eternal physical-chemical infinite pool, suggest that there would be ways such could be manipulated, but would we last long enough to have the tools? That is very much in question. Nevertheless after that, then the vision takes us to Type IV and beyond.

Type IV: is a universal civilization, capable of harnessing the energy of the whole universe. This civilization would be super galactic, able to travel throughout the entire universe and consume the energy output of several—possibly all—galaxies.

It would also be capable of projects of gargantuan proportions, such as manipulating space-time and tinkering with entropy, thus reaching immortality on a grand scale. It would be an essentially indestructible and highly utopian civilization."

Here, Pi set in. "Vicente, we of this panel have studied Forever, and we know it to be, everywhere as you reiterated a chemical-physical recycling entity.

So let us not be too uncertain that humans won't achieve these states. It all depends on how we work our way up to our most advanced stage, that which the Vistavien calls the Ultimate Humans. *It all depends on whether we can get along with each other, and that surely has to do with what is inside us, how our genetics drives our humanity from the ape-state."*

"Yes that is surely the case, although I am happy that I opened this up."   And, said Pi "We are too, it is that long term future that we will focus on, and you have laid out an important staging. "

"Thanks Dr. Pi, that is enough, though…I hope I have adequately sketched in the idea… Humans could progress way into the future, given many variables and the capture of sufficient energy, no questions as we see some of that. This covered says if we continue to exist we have rather awesome possibilities...I will not go on with 5-7, but those are proposed out there."

"Of course we do not really use yet use all of "Type I" civilization methods, although we do use nuclear power, and we use electrical flow to communicate and this, to me seems critically important to Human Evolution and is growing very fast! Moore's law reflects this!

It refers to an observation made by Intel co-founder Gordon Moore in 1965. He noticed that the number of transistors per square inch on integrated circuits had doubled every year since their invention. Moore's law predicts that this trend will continue into the foreseeable future."

Here Chandler, another computer oriented one of the panel enters. *"Now if we think of that PentaBox-Way-Back machine Vicente told of, with its power---we are forced to wonder about the overall evolutionary effect on us in growing cyberspace as it is clearly here!*

And so, it is important to remember that is our real and probable controlling evolution that is our computers and cyberspace. Is it not? I mean it is needed in the energy computation context, and seems to be everywhere and into everything else."

Pi entered with, "Yes, Chandler and Vicente, I see what is important here in a way, deeper. Perhaps we are coming, i.e., raising up the importance of the "Law of Complexity", or as it is sometimes called "Complex-Consciousness"!

Specifically, the Law-of Complex Consciousness is the postulated tendency of matter to become more complex over time and at the same time to become more conscious, more controlling. Shall we continue with that Professor?"

At this Dr. Why held up his hand (though there was a very pleased look on his face)!

"My goodness, this is getting interesting, and it seems it is heading toward a rational point, don't you think Vicente?

"Yes sir, I can see a focus, and I am very excited to delve into researching the subject fully."

"Great, as I would expect, unfortunately, it is getting good and late."

"Jane, Angelei, I know have some worries about kids. So I propose we take this up at the next Friday evening session."

"Remember crew it is a big day in the lab tomorrow, and that into next week…let's get some rest and back to the lab."

Here Dr.Why paused, and sort of wiping his brow commented.

"But, working it out of this evening revealed the path on which to focus I know all agree…we have much to chew on don't we? Exciting inquiries are on the horizon!"

CHAPTER 3.THE ENCOMPASING HUMAN MIND

It was actually three weeks later that the group could get together. There was much work in the lab on their man-made-living cells (BIOS+), because the membranes were being re-assayed as to amino acid content, and there were some family complications that arose. However, everyone was most anxious to meet and once again the panel paraded into the back room of the Newport Bar (and Grill) chatting with enthusiasm.

Tim and Pi, beer in hand, the rest with, well you know less alcoholic fare, a tomato juice here, and a ginger ale there…etc. Everyone seated…Pi started in.

"Remember team… we ended last meeting with the leading thought, the Law of "Complex-Consciousness".

This is really, really an important idea when it comes to Future Human Evolution!"

"And, it was put forward by thinkers in the very same times that Einstein was pushing his agenda. We should honor those thinkers, of course, again and again as they give perspectives on our lives and the future."

"Well the "The Law" was first formulated by the Jesuit priest and paleontologist Pierre Teilhard de Chardin in his 1955 work "The Phenomenon of Man"! Some of us remember Teilhard's thinking as having parallels with our mentors "Future Speak", that is, the teacher and Vistavien See-ela, as revealed to the Professor in his Fulbright in Africa.

So to put it in an easy to see flow…Teilhard held that… in all time and everywhere, matter is actually endeavoring to complexify upon itself, as is clearly observable in the evolutionary history of the Earth."

"Matter complexified from inanimate matter, to plant life, to animal life, to human life. Or, from the geosphere, to the biosphere, to what he and several other thinkers of this time referred to as the "Noosphere" (of which humans are centrally represented, because of their reality, possession of a consciousness which reflects upon themselves). That as most here know is "Dasein"!

As evolution rises through the geosphere, biosphere, and Noosphere, matter continues to rise in a continual increase of both complexity, consciousness, and adaptability!"

"The rates of this are in fact documentable"… Here, Pi passes around a display from the internet.

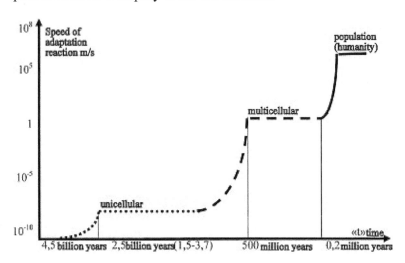

Then Pi relates. "This displays the evolution of the reaction rates (speed in adapting to situations) in (and for) living systems from the unicellular organism (ions through membranes), to multicellular (e.g. blood through vessels, momentum along nerve fibers) and in human populations, i.e. communications: sound (voice and audio, the speed of radio-electromagnetic waves, electric current, light, optical, tele-communications[1.])"

"To help here as we go along, the Anthrosphere has to do with what physically humans do to earth. This "Noosphere" which will be a most important subject for Vicente has to do with their united thoughts! In the terms of many 'The Global Brain'. In my terms, if you will, it is the "Encompassing Human Mind"!

For the priest Teilhard, more explicitly, the Law of "Complexity-Consciousness" continues to run on today in the form of the socialization of mankind!"

"Now, so as to emphasize an important relationship. The closed and circular surface of the Earth contributes to the increased compression (socialization) of mankind!"

"As human beings continue to come into closer contact with one another, their methods of interaction continue to complexify in the form of better (maybe higher is a more fitting word) organized social networks, which contributes to an overall increase in consciousness, or the "Noosphere".

What is most critical to us, we who focus on the future, is the healthy saving of humankind as this complexifies."

"Teilhard imagines a critical threshold, the so-called "Omega Point", in which mankind will have reached its highest point of complexification (socialization) and thus its highest point of consciousness."

"At this point in Teilhard's view, consciousness will rupture through time and space and assert itself on a higher plane of existence (a stellar one) from which, in Teilhard's thinking, it cannot come back."

---

1. This is display is simplified from Wikipedia in a section on the subject of the Noosphere.

"In Teilhard's view, because the Law of Complexity-Consciousness runs everywhere and at all times, and because of the immensity of both time and space and the immensity of the chances for matter to find the right conditions to complexify upon itself, it is highly probable that life exists, has existed, and will exist in the universe apart from our Earth. (This met with firm objections from his church.)"

"This of course is within the finding of our Forever Panel. The physical chemical makeup of Forever, necessarily leaving the possibilities of "Life" as nearly infinite and not including only us, though we may have come from "Such Other", i.e. following Fermi's paradox."

"However, to continue and clarify that unusual term…Noosphere (sometimes Noosphere') is the "Sphere of human thought". The word is derived from the Greek νοῦς (nous "mind") + σφαῖρα (sphaira "sphere"), in lexical analogy to "atmosphere" and "biosphere". This term was "first' introduced by Pierre Teilhard de Chardin as early as 1922 in his "Cosmogenesis".

It is important at the same time to note that there are others who thinking along the same line deserve attention and credit here. Thus, the first use of the term, may have come by Édouard Le Roy, who together with Chardin was listening to lectures of Vladimir Vernadsky at Sorbonne (We have discussed this thinker)."

"In 1936 Vernadsky presented the idea of the Noosphere in a letter to Boris Leonidovich Lichkov (though, he states that the concept derives from Le Roy). Citing the work of Teilhard's biographer Rene Cuenot. Even so, Sampson and Pitt stated that although the concept was jointly developed by all three men (Vernadsky, LeRoy, and Teilhard), Teilhard believed that he actually invented the word. He said, "I believe, so far as one can ever tell, that the word 'Noosphere' was my invention: but it was he [Le Roy] who launched it."

"Well, anyway, I suggest we reference mostly or at least always "Teilhard' to simplify our discussions, and so back to the theme and if you will in reference to the handout figure. …It gives a succinct view of our Universal evolution. Remember Tim gave us a backdrop with his BioGeo report."

"Having seen the ways in which the earth is affected by us, we may now consider in more detail, the idea of Universal Evolution involving the theory formulated by Pierre Teilhard de Chardin and Julian Huxley that describes the gradual development of the Universe from subatomic particles to human society, considered by Teilhard as the last stage!"

"Including Vernadsky's these thinkers' formulated very similar theories describing the gradual development of the universe from subatomic particles to human society and beyond. Teilhard's theories are better known in the West (and have also been commented on by Julian Huxley), and integrate Darwinian evolution and Christianity, whilst Vernadsky wrote more purely from a scientific perspective."

"Three classic levels are described. They are Cosmogenesis (Teilhard) or the formation of inanimate matter (the Physio sphere of Wilber), culminating in the Lithosphere, Atmosphere, Hydrosphere, etc. (Teilhard), or collectively, the Geosphere (Vernadsky). Here progress is ruled by structure and mechanical laws, and matter is primarily of the nature of non-consciousness (Teilhard - the "Without")."

"This is followed by Biogenesis (Teilhard) and the origin of life or the Biosphere (Vernadsky, Teilhard), where there is a greater degree of complexity and consciousness (Teilhard - the "Within"), Ecology (Vernadsky) comes into play, and progress and development is the result of Darwinian mechanisms of evolution." At this point Pi draws a breath, examins her audience, smiles pleasently and continues...

…."Finally, a main point, there is human evolution and the rise of thought or cognition (Vernadsky, Teilhard), and a further leap in complexity and the interior life or consciousness (Teilhard), resulting in the birth of the Noosphere (Vernadsky, Teilhard). "

"Just as the biosphere transformed the geosphere, so the Noosphere (human intervention) transformed the biosphere (Vernadsky). Here the evolution of human society (socialization) is ruled by active psychological, economic, informational and essential Communicative Processes."

"For Teilhard there is a further stage, one of spiritual evolution, the Christing of the collective Noosphere, in which humanity converges in a single divinization as mentioned that he calls the Omega Point!"

Great Pi! Dr.Why interjects, "That surely sets for us an important stage. That is the earth's spherical structure, delimits humans to increasing interrelation via our communication, into as you put it, "Encompassing Human Mind" or in Teilhard's words the Noosphere.

Vicente the Professor asks... Could you at the next meeting amplify Pi's introduction. And, of course, carry us into some theory as to how this all may impact the forward evolution of Mankind, with a bit of our evolutionary history.

For now group let's all see to those various home matters that must be taken care of, as I know in the end---well we are just "present humans".

Present humans, yes! But, it must be said they have challenged themselves to consider the far distant future for your forthcoming children, something that few, soaked in the collective insanities of the present are not considering at all!"

……………………………..

Gathered next Friday night, all minds cleared from the pressures of daily needs, the pursuit into Future Human Evolution was on again. On the Doctor's previous instruction… Vicente chooses to start with the topic of our "Evolutionary Stages".

He begins with "I will get us underway, a bit will be a repeat of some that Pi introduced, i.e. we will return to the "Noosphere"." There are actually nine levels described in the literature for "Universal Evolution". The "classical" biological stages conclude with levels 6, 7 & 8 within complete universal evolution. Stages 1 to 5 are grouped into the Lithosphere, also called Geosphere or Physiosphere, where the structure of organisms is ruled by mechanical laws and coincidence. Stages 6 to 8 are grouped into the Biosphere, where the structure of the organisms is ruled by genetical mechanisms. Then stage 9, the one called *"Noosphere"*, where the structure of human society (socialization) is ruled by the three processes psychological, informational and communicative!

For the *Noosphere* the prime reference is Teilhard's Book "The Phenomenon of Man". The Noosphere (/ˈnoʊ.əsfɪər/; sometimes noösphere) is in my estimation easiest to "think of 'as the *"Sphere of Human Thought"*.

The word to be specific derives from the Greek νοῦς (nous "mind") and σφαῖρα (sphaira "sphere"), in lexical analogy to "atmosphere" and "biosphere".

As said, it was introduced by Pierre Teilhard de Chardin in 1922 in his Cosmogenesis. Another possibility as has been covered is that the first use of the term was by Édouard Le

Roy (1870–1954), who together with Teilhard was listening to lectures of at the Sorbonne. In 1936, Vernadsky accepted the idea of the Noosphere in a letter to Boris Leonidovich Lichkov (though he states that the concept derives from Le Roy).

Just as this was said the Professor received a phone call from one of the lab technicians, Johan. "Well, sorry Vicente-Folks, looks like we will have to discontinue, seems the power was out at the School of Medicine, and our lab is without power in the incubators, we will all have to rush there and put the generator into action to save the incubations."

~~~~~~

The rescue mission for the BioSims+ was partially successful, such that near late stage cells were saved in sufficient numbers to continue experiments. The lab, however, was not fully up to power so most of the staff was given leave for personal time.

Vicente took advantage to deepen his studies and to find rooming. There was not much available so he settled for an efficiency apartment in a rather rundown neighborhood, but at a price he could afford.

Pi and Tim on this 'leave' were able to work on something magic for themselves, that is, their wedding! This was to all in the group sometimes thought to be a bit of a flight of fancy that they would really get married, though a union was suspected from those 'close encounters' in the lab. One reason for the surprise was that Pi is oriental, and Tim is a Jewish man (yet still hunting for foundation). So the ceremony was in the end, as promised, to be one very unusual, Jewish in basic vows but, with oriental décor!

Chandler and Jane, took the time to communicate with the kids teachers, as it was near term end. And they were pleased that their offspring were doing well, except for young James who seemed to visit the principal's office a good deal. The pair was also dealing with the lingering intestinal illness that Chandler acquired on the India "Forever Retreat".

Jehan took the opportunity to return to Pakistan to visit with her adopted father who had saved her after the terrorist attack at the Institute in India where she had attended school.

The Professor had this time to consider his potential retirement, and a probable new replacement.

And Skellan, Angelei and Gabriel took the time to tour the Princeton Campus, showing Alexander, yes even so young, the various facilities, and they were sure to take him to the home where Albert Einstein lived. Skellan filled in for the boy as they looked at the rather traditional house. Herr Doctor Professor Einstein lived from 1879 to 1955. He first visited Princeton in 1921, the year before he received the Nobel Prize. He was here at Princeton to deliver five "Stafford Little" lectures on the theory of relativity and to accept an honorary degree. He returned again in 1933 as a life member of the newly founded "Institute for Advanced Study" and lived here for the remaining twenty-two years of his life. One of my favorite quotes by this genius is "We cannot solve our problems by the same thinking that created them". To which the boy said, "You would think most people would realize that" which prompted his brother Gabriel to lift the boy with a hug---expostulating... Oh how much we wished they did!

CHAPTER 4: A STUDENT'S LEGACY

In their next meetings, Vicente expanded extensively on the concept of and factors effecting the Future Evolution of Humans, at first stressing theory, such as the following...

..."In the theory of Vernadsky, the Noosphere is the third in a succession of phases of development of the Earth, after the geosphere (inanimate matter) and the biosphere (biological life). Just as the emergence of life fundamentally transformed the geosphere, he argued that the emergence of human cognition is that which is fundamentally responsible for transforming the biosphere.

In contrast to the conceptions of the Gaia theorists and the promoters of cyberspace, Vernadsky's Noosphere emerges at the point where humankind, through the mastery of nuclear processes, begins to create its necessary resources through the transmutation of elements. This thinking is as so many subjects concerning the Noosphere currently being researched as part of the "Princeton Global Consciousness Project".

In contrast to that line of thinking, Teilhard perceived a directionality in evolution along an axis of increasing Complexity/Consciousness. For Teilhard, the *Noosphere is the sphere of thought encircling the earth that has emerged through evolution as a consequence of this growth in complexity in consciousness."*

"The Noosphere is therefore as much part of nature as the barysphere, lithosphere, hydrosphere, atmosphere, and biosphere. As a result, Teilhard sees the "social phenomenon as the culmination of and not the lessening of the biological phenomenon." These social phenomena are part of the

Noosphere and include, for example, legal, educational, religious, research, industrial and technological systems."

"In this sense, the Noosphere emerges through and is constituted by the interaction of human minds! The Noosphere thus grows in step with the organization of the human mass in relation to itself as it populates the earth."

Here Jane a catholic contributed. "I learned that Teilhard argued the Noosphere evolves towards ever greater personalization, individuation and unification of its elements. And deep in his understanding he saw the Christian notion of love as being the principal driver of oogenesis."

To this Vicente contributed. "Although a Catholic he remarks that this sees love as the driver, i.e. the human sense of benevolence and caring essential as Omega is approached, and it is the primary workings inside the Noosphere to achieve the most beautiful ascent into eternity. Although he may have as priest, by a kind of default, imply Christianity as the driver, he certainly recognized that there are a great many philosophies, and faiths that center on love for each other."

"With love as the driver the theory is that evolution would culminate in that time called the Omega Point---an apex of thought/consciousness which he as a Christian representative identified with the eschatological return of Christ." *Yet, this same apex of thought/consciousness could be applied to all faiths if they are in union of accepting each other and solidly standing on their benevolent beginnings. Further, it must be commented that without that basic operation of humanity for all peoples, whatever their faith, there can be no Stellar end at the Omega Point."*

Also, Vernadsky's clear minded idea, nuclear conversion to substantiate the species could be categorized the same. That is, in short, our long term evolution could head toward a magnificent culmination, if correctly matured through collaboration of all human communities!"

"I like to think of this as the complete human soul coalescing into the stars, belonging to Forever!"

"But all of this has a "Catch Twenty-Two', if you will allow me to use that well-worn phrase. We need to keep in mind that there will be an end, why should it be a disaster?"

The Future Navigator Panel at this, of course, nodded agreement one to the next. They understood through research what the character of Forever is and how important our record in that must become. After some discussion on that, Vicente continued…

…"Well, one of the original aspects concerning the Noosphere does indeed deal with evolution."

"Henri Bergson, with his L'évolution créatrice (1907), was one of the first to propose evolution is "creative" and cannot necessarily be explained solely by Darwinian natural selection. L'évolution créatrice is upheld, according to Bergson, by a constant vital force which animates life and fundamentally connects mind and body, an idea opposing the dualism of René Descartes."

"In 1923, C. Lloyd Morgan took this work further, elaborating on an "emergent evolution". This could explain increasing complexity including the evolution of mind, which I would submit is now in our more complete understanding, right before us, in our knowledge of the evolutionary steps from Homo habilis to sapiens."

"Morgan found many of the most interesting changes in living things have been in some cases largely discontinuous with past evolution. Therefore, these living things did not necessarily evolve only through a gradual process of natural selection. Rather, he posited, the process of evolution experiences (experiential) jumps in complexity (such as the emergence of a self-reflective universe, or Noosphere). "

"So one can say complexification of human cultures, particularly language, facilitated a quickening or jump in evolution in which cultural evolution occurs more rapidly than biological evolution."

"Concequently, recent understanding of the human impact on the biosphere have led to a link between the notions of critical co-evolution---that is a forced harmonization of biological and cultural evolution." And of course, cultural evolution today is heavily steeped in the rapid evolution of our communication. (accelerated communication, could lead to accelerated biological changes in our future and to our behavior.)

"So there is clear rational in my thinking regards dissertation content. I wish to emphasize, that subject i.e. the increasing volume of communication in cyberspace, which in effect is the allowance for humans to place (uninhibited, perhaps counter humanitarian) thoughts into computer language!"

So it was this aspect-computer driven communication-its effect on Human Evolution that Vicente proposed to bear on in our future meetings.

And this evolved, his development of it, over the semester. He spent most of his seminar time explaining the way the internet is designed and how it reaches virtually everyone on the planet. His thoroughness left no stone in electronic communication unturned, the panel without the advantage of a degree could still have been awarded one if tested - the teaching was so complete!

Even so, reaching home one evening near the end of the semester Vicente noticed down the street under a street lamp four or five people holding baseball bats! Then the next night he saw the crowd had grown. He felt the hair on the nape of his next stand on end, because he had seen that before! In his childhood in a similar neighborhood, the youths in gangs, often came to seedy and deadly ends after such night time confrontations!

And, indeed there was an unbelievable and horrible, tragic event and unbelievable loss. Vicente is killed, an innocent bystander - in that gang- related situation! This kind and brilliant man was killed while getting out of his car. He lay in the street shot twice, for hours before someone called for help, and although transported to the hospital by the EMTs, he passed away well before reaching the Emergency Room!

When the trouble was brewing, being a proactive man, he was concerned about his safety and he hurried to complete the writing and get his "dissertation proposal" to Pi and Tim, whom he rightfully viewed as his "Personal Teaching Assistants'.

The afternoon of the incident, He met them in the lab, described his concerns and with a courage that Tim and Pi greatly admired, exclaimed it was just a caution.

Yet, when he returned home that evening, just at his front door, getting out of his car, he was gunned down. Although the crowds he worried about had formed, he was killed in a drive by shooting. And this was the fate also of three of those under the lamp post.

The death of Vicente was beyond understanding for the lab staff. For Gabriel who knew this man once in the Navy as fellow Navy Corpsman and friend, it was deeply disturbing, leading him (with Pi in support) to investigate the killing and find restitution, which he accomplishes, working with the police and tracing the shooters.

There are no words to describe the distress and atmosphere, the overwhelming deep angry feelings at the funeral. For all those in the group it was truly crushing this loss of such an intelligent and gentle man, and this from a group who investigated and understood life and death deeper than most. Knowing the pain himself, the Professor gave his administrative staff and the group a week off. Most, though continued to work although they consulted the University Grief Counselor.

In time, that is in the new academic year a new student was accepted to replace Vicente. She entered the group as a laboratory assistant with prospects to pursue a doctorate. This is Chivonn Washington who has as Vicente a Master of Science Degree in Computer Science. After all get to know her, and find her most dependable, indeed she is especially intelligent, she is given Vicente's files and assigned to continue his series of reports. To help her synchronize with the group's overall mission, Jehan also gives her some insight into the "Vistaviens" teaching and provides a copy of the group's books, including "The Edge of Forever. From her interest, daily obvious---in questions and comments, it is suspected that she will most likely assume Vicente's line of research and take on a similar dissertation.

So it is that Vicente's inquiry into our Evolutionary Future, is not lost. The following account will present the essence of Vicente's assessment but as reported by Chivonn.

Being one of her first assignments it is noted that Chivonn will quote directly from the document, but selecting as she sees most needed.

She is in fact well qualified to step into Vicente's place as she was a fellow M.S. student with him, and the group could not help but hear the quiver in her voice, the first time she began to report his work, tears in her eyes. Here, following, is the way she prefaces and continues to report the work.

"As I found it, the total construction of his work is already formed as a valid dissertation! That is, the expected dissertation design is present. It contains an abstract, an introductory chapter with statement of the problem that begins the work containing hypothesis and delimitations.

There is a literature review chapter, there is a chapter on research design and methodology, a chapter detailing analysis and findings follows that, and his last chapter is appropriately a summary, giving conclusions, with discussions and recommendations. The final references section is massive and comprehensive!

In net, the work, the core of Vicente's dissertation reviews causation for and potential solutions to problems regarding reaching Omega that carry Teilhard's proposal to its consideration limits. It seems to me that Vicente provided us all the words which are appropriate to include background, history, objectives, research line for any dissertation using the Teilhard propositions.

Although he centers on Teilhard, he does give credence to other notions of our developing Noosphere, or as used much in the work "Our Global Brain." I probably do sound biased but to me it is a truly scholarly work. Here is the critical introductory statement.

"The notion of the Noosphere must now- in post Teilhard days be subdivided and expanded and those aspects be set into the expectations and solutions for the future." He continues… *"We must realize he spoke a great truth, and take the basic idea of our Noosphere to its logical-course of consideration and describe the necessary to insure its successful final outcome!.* His document then proceeds in traditional, yes, the expected dissertation form. However, I am handing out an introductory outline in summary language but using dissertation components. That is, I have compiled his information much as one would for a Journal Article and I will report relative to that, rather than reading the full document. So to read…first the outline.

Toward full consideration, the following topics expand on Teilhard's hypothesis to a necessary degree, and develop a "Solution Path."

A. Post Teilhard Considerations
    1. Evolution of the Intellect
    2. Cyberspace, its fateful connection
    3. Hypercyclic Morphogenesis, self-reproduction
    4. Infosphere, the practiced gathering of opinions
    5. The Ideosphere, routinely applying generic ideas

B. Potential Problems from Apparent Solutions
    1. Noocracy, powerful gathering, potential commanding
    2. Consequence illustrations.
        a. Computational predictability
        b. Control and potential wayward outcomes
        c. Learning from Mimetics

C. Resolution (Fight Fire with Fire)
    1. Protect the Future via an "Omega Shield"
        a. Recognize the Starter "Cy-gene"
    2. Shield the Cy-gene
        a. Reality Aware Cyber Humans via Ideologies
            Objective Humanism
            Self-Actuating Development
            Mind Centered Openness

Now using the outline, from here I read sections as I excerpted them following an order that was presented in logical sequencing...

"Evolution of the Intellect

The idea of the Noosphere expresses a result, not, other than complexity-consciousness, a detailed mechanism.

However, in recent times that investigation has been discussed. And, realizing the potential for troubling turns there are serious concerns driving such studies.

In 2005 Alexey Eryomin proposed a new concept related to the Noosphere which is imbedding a deeper description. We might say to coin a related term there is an "Oogenesis" in understanding the evolution of intellectual systems, concepts of intellectual systems, information logistics, information speed, intellectual energy, and intellectual potential. In short all of this may be consolidated into a *"Theory of the Intellect"*.

This theory combines the biophysical parameters of intellectual energy to the amount of information, its acceleration (frequency, speed) and the distance it's being sent. This idea has for some reflective scientist thought to be amendable into a formula, although that has not yet reached prominence.

Even so, according this newer idea there is a *progressive evolution of Homo sapiens mind*! This derives rationally from the analogy between the human brain with its enormous amount of neural cells firing at the same time and a similarly functioning hyper-active human society. *To wit, the brain cannot help but assimilate that which is all around it and constantly bombarding it.* Two graphs constructed by the author and included in Vicente's work illustrate the idea. These are on the handout I have just distributed. (here below)

This is a hypothesis that might be roughly compared philosophically somewhat like recapitulation theory which links the evolution of the human brain to the development of human civilization. The theory of the intellect, though relates specifically to cognitive development, i.e. the parallel is between the amount of people living on Earth and the amount of neurons becoming more and more obvious in real effect, leading us to viewing global intelligence as in an analogy for the human brain.

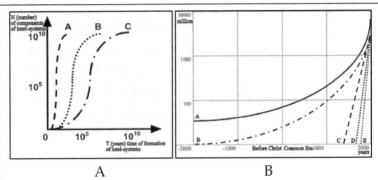

A   B

Graph A. Iteration of the number of components in Intellectual systems. A - Number of neurons in the brain during individual development (ontogenesis), B - number of people (evolution of populations of humanity), C - number of neurons in the nervous systems of organisms during evolution (phylogenies).

Graph B. Emergence and evolution of info-interactions within populations of Humanity. A - world human population → 7 billion ; B - number of literate persons; C – number of reading books (with beginning of printing); D - number of receivers (radio, TV); E - number of phones, computers, Internet users

Although there are such hypotheses on the ongoing development of the human mind, it is a simple, real factual observation that all of the people living on this planet have undoubtedly inherited the amazing cultural treasures of the past, be it production, social and intellectual ones. *That is, quite directly, we are genetically hardwired to be a sort of "live RAM" of the global intellectual system!*

In net, Alexey Eryomin argues that humanity is moving inescapably towards a unified self-contained informational and intellectual system. His research has shown the probability of "Super Intellect" realizing itself as "Global Intelligence on Earth"! (The Global Brain)

In his document Vicente agrees with the following statement by those reporting this "Evolution of the Intellect". "We could get closer to understanding the most profound patterns and laws of the Universe if these kinds of research were given enough attention. The resemblance between the individual human's mind development and that of the whole human race has to be explored further if we are to face some of the threats to humanity in the future." Then Vicente postulates his most serious and central concern namely the effect of Cyberspace on human development – its intellect. That is a major issue to focus on regarding our evolution in the future. "

Cyberspace it's Fateful Connection

To continue that from Vicente he addresses specific concerns emanating from Cyberspace…"At this point, in time much further than the original Teilhard proposal, it must be recognized that our evolution is dependent on cyberspace outcomes, (which, arguments can be made, later in this document, are embedding in our brain DNA)."

"Formally, cyberspace is "the notational environment in which communication over computer networks occurs."

The term was first used in science fiction and cinema in the 1980s, was adopted by computer professionals and became a household term in the1990s. During this period, the uses of the internet, networking, and digital communication were all growing dramatically and the term "cyberspace" was able to represent the many new ideas and phenomena that were emerging. The term is clearly appropriate as a blanket one for reference as to effects into future human behavior as the Noosphere continues to expand. That is, the notion of a Global Brain naturally must include the ever enfolding prevalent communication.

A major question wound around this is, where are we with Cyberspace and what pathways could be opened in relation to the Noosphere and the Omega point?

It is important to recall the depth in this consideration, which now is on a daily practiced-market basis."

"Today there are companies specialized in developing and deploying as expressed in company language "semantic solutions for information management and intelligence information analysis and sharing". What they do is sell software that allows computers and people to collect, organize, and keep current critical data regarding people, places, events, and various types of personal entities."

"These marketed solutions are at face for contingency preparedness and response, public safety and crime prevention, and defense and national security, yet the open market, technology advance, hacking and various ways of capturing coding---for such services is sweeping, as many who have experienced virus, and hostage crashed computer will testify. So it is via such packages possible to glean "mental false implants" toward population behavior."

From here Vicente described...first something called "Hypercyclic Morphogenesis", then he cited some important "Mimetic Headings" as in the literature. These are the Ideosphere, Infosphere, Noocracy, and an example of the power of computers holding information, which he called a few examples of "The Implantsphere".

I will read from these discussions all quoting directly...

Hypercyclic Morphogenesis

Hypercyclic morphogenesis refers to the emergence of a higher order of self-reproducing structure or organization and hierarchy within a system. It involves combining the idea of the hypercycle with that of morphogenesis.

The hypercycle involves, i.e. resembles a problem in biochemistry. It mimics that of molecules combining in a self-reacting group which is able to stay together (like genetic molecules for example). It is posited thus as the foundation for the emergence of multi-cellular organisms.

The researcher Thompson saw morphogenesis as a central part of the development of an organism as cell differentiation led to new organs appearing as it develops and grows. The chemistry and mathematics involved in such a process, would also be studied mathematically in the formulation of catastrophe theory.

Nevertheless, it can be argued that such a thing as Hypercyclic morphogenesis is a real, out-coming from human mentality. It is occurring today, slowly yielding a certain human persona! Those in "senior citizen status" know this, seeing the change in the way people, think, accept more and more unacceptable actions and behave!

On the societal level, Rosser suggested applications are visible in political economy such as the actual emergence of the European Union out of the conscious actions of the leaders of its constituent nation states, or the appearance of a higher level governance in urban hierarchy during economic development. It has been applied to the emergence of higher levels in ecologic-economic systems in turn augmenting the Noosphere of Vernadsky.

In short, we are, in reality, an experience within a mental Hypercyclic Morphogenesis!

Ideosphere

Semantics experts' note that the "Ideosphere", much like the Noosphere, is in a realm of "memetic evolution" just like the biosphere is the realm of biological evolution. The term, even so, is convenient in relating human actuality.

It is the "place" where thoughts, theories and ideas are created, evaluated and evolved.

The Ideosphere though is not considered to be a physical place by most people. It is instead "inside the minds" of all the humans in the world!

There is a technical distinction. It is also, sometimes, believed that the Internet, books and other media could be considered to be part of the Ideosphere. Alas, as such media are not (perhaps with exception of some developing media means as AI) "self-aware", it (the Ideosphere) cannot process the thoughts it contains as humans who have Dasein.

According to philosopher Yasuhiko Kimura, the Ideosphere is in the form of a "concentric Ideosphere" where ideas are generated by a few people with others merely perceiving and accepting these ideas from these "external authorities." We need think of this, that there is behind the matter the question, how deeply can it be centered, and perhaps more important, can it be within as we start life, i.e. an "Engram"!

Kaimura, hopefully, advocates in his terms an "Omni centric Ideosphere" where all individuals create new ideas and interact as self-authorities.

Vicente notes this self-authority is important to further human development, which will be touched later when defensive mechanisms are relayed.

As said the use of the mimetic term "Ideosphere" has a foundation. The aspects of Memetics important to consider in relation to the Noosphere are addressed later. However, mimetics is the theory of mental content based on an analogy with Darwinian evolution, as originating from Richard Dawkins' 1976 book "The Selfish Gene". Proponents describe Memetics as an approach to evolutionary models of cultural information transfer. That is, the mimetic mind can certainly grow via survival evolution!

Infosphere

Into the proposals of thoughts held growing from one person to the next, are two fold realities. These are the Infosphere and the Noocracy.

The "Infosphere" is a neologism (coinage, new word) composed of information and sphere. The word refers to an environment, much like a biosphere, that is populated by informational entities called "Inforgs".

While an example of the sphere of information is that in cyberspace---Infospheres are not necessarily limited to purely online environments. (However, the notion of a Cybersphere is relevant as what is in the Infosphere, will as we have seen with the Way-Back machine, be fodder for its hold.)

The first documented use of the word "Infosphere" was a 1971 Time Magazine book review by R.Z. Sheppard in which he writes *"In much the way that fish cannot conceptualize water or birds the air, man barely understands his Infosphere, that encircling layer of electronic and typographical smog composed of clichés from journalism, entertainment, advertising and government."*

In 1980 it was used by Alvin Toffler in his book "The Third Wave" in which he writes "What is inescapably clear, whatever we choose to believe, is that we are altering our Infosphere fundamentally. In fact, we are adding a whole new strata of communication to the social system!

The emerging "Third Wave Infosphere" makes that of the Second Wave era - dominated by its mass media, the post office, and the telephone---seem hopelessly primitive by contrast"!

The Toffler definition proved prophetic as the use of "Infosphere" in the 1990s expanded beyond simple media to "speculate about" to the *in-common evolution of the Internet, Society and Culture!*

In his book "Digital Dharma", Steven Vedro writes, "Emerging from what French philosopher-priest Pierre Teilhard de Chardin called the shared Noosphere of collective human thought, invention and spiritual seeking, the Infosphere is sometimes used to conceptualize a field that engulfs our physical, mental and etheric bodies; it affects our dreaming and our cultural life. *Our evolving nervous system has been extended! As media sage Marshall McLuhan predicted in the early 1960s, into a Global Embrace!"*

The term Infosphere (as Global Embrace) has also been used by Luciano Floridi Professor of Philosophy and Ethics of Information at the University of Oxford on the basis of biosphere, to denote the whole informational environment constituted by all the informational entities (thus including informational agents as well), their properties, interactions, processes and mutual relations. It is an environment comparable to, but in a way different from cyberspace (which is one of its guiding regions, as it were), since it also includes off-line and analogue spaces of information.

According to Floridi, *it is possible to equate the Infosphere to the totality of being!*

Suggesting this leads him into an informational ontology. That is investigation into the nature and relations of being. Hence, among the many considerations is the "Manipulation of the Infosphere", and some special notions on "Publication of the Infosphere".

Manipulation of the Infosphere. The manipulation of the Infosphere is subject to a metaphysical analysis[1] and its rules. Information is considered to be Shannon[2] and is treated in a physical sense separate from energy and matter (hard reality).

The manipulations into the Infosphere include the erasing, transfer, duplication, and destruction of information.

~~~~~~

1. Metaphysics is a branch of philosophy investigating the fundamental nature of reality. Example, "What is it like?"
2. Shannon Information theory studies the quantification, storage, and communication of information. It was originally proposed by Claude E. Shannon in 1948 to find fundamental limits on signal processing and communication operations such as data compression, in a landmark paper entitled "A Mathematical Theory of Communication".

Vicente, illustrates this in his document with a number of examples, drawn from recent news, as the president making statements that have no proof but the transfer is accepted by many uniformed about the foundation of facts. It has thus a way of supporting bias and bigotry.

That is the Infosphere can be (and is) used to cement ideas that by in large induce destructive behavior!

<u>Publications Using Infosphere.</u> Publications concerning the term Infosphere do range from commercial to visionary, to real possibilities.

For example, the IBM Software Group created the Infosphere brand in 2008 for its Information Management software products.

In the animated sitcom Futurama, the Infosphere is a huge sphere floating in space, in which a species of giant talking---floating brains attempts to store all of the information known in the universe.

Much more of concern and now some argue permeating in the world of reality, this term "Infosphere" was used by Dan Simmons in the science-fiction saga "Hyperion" (published 1989) to indicate what the Internet could become in the future: a place parallel, virtual, formed of billions of networks, with "artificial life" on various scales, from what is equivalent to an insect (small programs) to what is equivalent to a god (artificial intelligences), whose motivations are diverse, seeking to both help mankind and harm it!

This very salient notion is pointing to the probability that simulated reality could become reality (of behavior)?

How could that happen? There are several avenues to it but it would be guided...via a forceful source of information!

Noocracy

And Vicente answers that as follows. "We will call that force for purpose here, the "Noocracy". It is one in relation to the Noosphere, so it is appropriately termed the "Noocracy".

Well, forceful would be a simple way of expressing it or the "Aristocracy of the Wise", as defined by Plato. However, this is not about kings and queens, it is a social and political system that is *"based on the priority of the human mind"*, according to Vladimir Vernadsky. And, it was also further developed in the writings of Pierre Teilhard de Chardin!

As to etymology, the word itself is derived from Greek nous, Gen. Noos (νους) meaning "mind" or "intellect", and "kratos" (κράτος), "authority" or "power"! This, on the positive side is what the Vistavien (the mentor of the Future Navigators) wants. That is, the Mind under Self-Control, free to interpret and make good decisions. But, of course, she meant free in the open minded sense, so that rational decisions can prevail!

One of the first attempts to implement such a political system as a Noocracy was perhaps Pythagoras' "City of the Wise" one that he planned to build in Italy together with his followers, in the order of "Mathematikoi".

In modern history, similar concepts were introduced by Vladimir Vernadsky, who did not use this term however, but the term "Noosphere.

As defined by Plato, Noocracy is considered to be the future political system for the entire human race, but replacing Democracy ("the authority of the crowd") and other forms of government. Obviously, with our lessons from Cesare to Hitler to the dictators of the day, that can be manipulated in an adverse manner, and the tool is potentially there in the "Infosphere" and that through the massively expanding Cybersphere.

Mikhail Epstein defined Noocracy this way, *"As the thinking matter increases its mass in nature (just as the geo- and biosphere) it grows into the Noosphere, hence, the future of humanity can be envisioned as potentially a Noocracy, that is, the power of the collective brain controls, rather than separate individuals representing certain social groups or society as whole.* This is extremely concerning! The question is what would that collective brain be, how would it come about? It surely would effect Human Evolution!

In the European Commission Community Research article, "Art & Scientific Research are Free: Towards a Culture of Life", it states several commentaries by Hans Jonas and especially Ladislav Kovác about Noocracy.

"If Plato called his conception of governments a "sophocracy," then, we can envision (as seen by these authors) for Noocracy a modern ideal! That is a political system characterized by social experimentation with a scientific institutionalized base that could be called a "Noocracy."

"Noocracy would not be the reign of the philosopher-king as seen in Plato. Nor would it be governed by science or the scientists. Yet, certainly one hopes for an ideal outcome.

Ideally, a power acquired and maintained according to the laws of competition, would remain in the hands of the political elites but with these elites being professionally trained, making the most of the analysis, the forecasts and the propositions emanating from a vast array of advisory groups made up of experts from all areas of science, and setting up fieldwork experiments."

These authors take for example the current controversy about genetically modified food or GMO, a textbook case about setting up such a policy.

"Within a (ideal) Noocracy in its own right, GMO would be tested in one or several areas or nations and scientifically monitored by all, under the guidance of a main administration body. With, at the end of the day, the costs and profits equitably shared by all. The principle of precaution, highly controversial at the present time, would then be applied, without slowing-down nor impeding the implementation of scientific inventions."

A this point in the presentation, Pi commented, "This is an example of Future Navigators working in the Noosphere if it were to be unfolding ideally, i.e. in as spirit of Objective Humanism". However, although the outcomes could be good for long term Human Evolution it sort of seems like communism, does it not? It seems as though it could go way wrong, become over dictating and that could be guided against Humanism.[1]

Problems from Apparent Solutions

"Yes, Pi (entered Chivonn) and Vicente is quick to address this." He said, "Noocracy, like technocracies, have been criticized for meritocratic failings, such as upholding of a non-egalitarian aristocratic ruling class. Others have upheld more democratic ideals as better epistemic models of law and policy. However, even though a potential useful guide to

1. The Navigators posit "Objective Humanism as a path to the Future. It is described in the books, "The Future Navigator" and its sequel "Navigators on the Edge of Forever".

human behavior, there is, indeed, a critical question, what actual way would it go in reality, given the power of the Cybersphere, that is without some forward consideration?"

Chivonn notes as her presentation is about to proceed further that Vicente first cites examples of the power of computers contributing to Cyberspace and then he gives examples of the intrusion into human endeavors. First she reads on the former in Vicente's words…

"And that concern is real. Indeed, the power of computers, i.e. operation in Cybersphere in ways that can influence opinion and outcomes are rather prolific."

"Computational Power: Here (as cited by Vicente) are examples of the developing power of cyberspace control".

"First should be considered is the computational means of control. Very soon the old means of computing will yield to the new, which is the "Quantum Computer". Quantum computing is as different from traditional computing as an abacus is from a MacBook. "Classical computing was invented in the 1940s. This is like that creation in way, but even far beyond it," says Scott Crowder of IBM Systems."

"Quantum computers are made up of parts called qubits, also known as quantum bits. Quantum superposition is most important because it allows the qubit to do two things at once. While traditional computers put bits in 0 and 1 configurations to calculate steps, a qubit can be a 0 and a 1 at the same time. Quantum entanglement, another purely quantum property, takes the possibilities a step further by intertwining the characteristics of two different qubits, allowing for even more calculations. Calculations that would take longer than a human's life span to work out on a classic computer can be completed in a matter of days or hours!"

"Eventually, quantum computing could outperform the world's fastest supercomputer—and then all computers ever made, combined.

What problems could be so complicated they would require a quantum computer? Here is an example. One to two percent of the world's energy is consumed per year for mass production of fertilizer. However, the quantum computer alone has the power to take care of this"

"There's a type of cyanobacteria that uses an enzyme to do nitrogen fixation at room temperature, which means it uses energy far more efficiently than industrial methods. "It's been too challenging for classical computer systems to date to work out how to use it but quantum computers would be able to reveal the enzyme's secrets immediately so researchers could re-create the process synthetically!

Pharmaceutical science could also benefit. One of the limitations to developing better, cheaper drugs is problems that arise when dealing with electronic structures. The ability to predict how molecules react with other drugs, and the efficacy of certain catalysts in drug development, could drastically speed up the pace of pharmaceutical development and, ideally, lower prices.

Finance is also plagued by complicated problems. Quantum computing could figure out the optimal way to rebalance portfolios day by day (or minute by minute) since that will require a computing power beyond the current potential of digital computers."

"While business applications within quantum computing are mostly hopeful theories, there's one area where experts agree quantum could be valuable: optimization. Using quantum computing to create a program that "thinks" through how to make business operations faster, smarter and cheaper could revolutionize countless industries. For example, quantum computers could be used to organize delivery truck routes so holiday gifts arrive faster during the rush before Christmas. They could take thousands of self-driving cars and organize them on the highway so all the drivers get to their destination via the fastest route. They could create automated translating software so international businesses don't have to bother with delays caused from translating emails."

"In net, the existing power of computers upon which cyberspace operates will in human future become so far much more capable that it cannot even be imagined!

While that can create applications making human time vastly more convenient, there is a flip side that should in rational minds be considered! Even now these flip side effects are able to predict and some even being seen.

For example, using algorithms partially modeled on the human brain, (a very important aspect to observe) researchers from the Massachusetts Institute of Technology have enabled computers to predict the immediate future by examining a photograph of humans doing this or that!"

"A program created at MIT's "Computer Science and Artificial Intelligence Laboratory" essentially watched two million online videos and observed how different types of scenes typically progress: people walk across golf courses, wave's crash on the shore, and so on. Now, when it sees a new still image, it can generate a short video clip (roughly 1.5 seconds long) showing its vision of the immediate future!"

"It's a system that tries to learn what plausible videos are ---what are plausible motions you might see," says Carl Vondrick, a graduate student at the laboratory and lead author on a research paper presented at the "Neural Information Processing Systems Conference" in Barcelona. The team aims to generate longer videos with more complex scenes in the future."

"But Vondrick says applications could one day go beyond turning photos into computer-generated format for image files that supports both animated and static images (GIFs). The system's ability to predict normal behavior could help spot unusual happenings in security footage or improve the reliability of self-driving cars, he says."

"If the system spots something unusual, like an animal of it has seen before running into the road, Vondrick explains that the vehicle "can detect the threat in that, evaluate and say, 'Okay, I've seen this situation before! I can let the driver take over!"(Vicenti says, so comforted will the driver do that?)

"To create the program, the MIT team relied on a scientific technique called deep learning that's become central to modern artificial intelligence research!"

<u>"Artificial Intelligence</u>: It's the approach that lets digital assistants like Apple's Siri and Amazon's Alexa understand what users want, and that drives image search and facial recognition advancements at Facebook and Google. "

Here Chivonn sets down the notes from which she is reading (taken from Vicente's dissertation) and comments extemporaneously, "And, yes, I understand that our BioSims Lab, Dr. Jodyn's, that is, uses artificial intelligence to predict what chemicals could be toxic to the cells they are creating." "To which, on behalf of the panel, Jehan nodded, and commented straight away, "yes, that is the case, and it is an important part of the work."

Chivonn, pleased with that input, continued…"Well, to return, as it turns out, experts say deep learning, which uses mathematical structures called Neural Networks (indeed used by the Jordyn Lab) to pull patterns from massive sets of data, could soon let computers make diagnoses from medical images, detect bank fraud, predict customer order patterns, and operate vehicles at least as well as people."

"Deep neural networks are performing better than humans on all kinds of significant problems, like image recognition, for example," says Chris Nicholson, CEO of a San Francisco firm which develops deep learning software and offers consulting. "Without them, I think self-driving cars would be a danger on the roads, but with them, self-driving cars are safer than human drivers."

"Neural networks take low-level inputs, like the pixels of an image or snippets of audio, and run them through a series of virtual layers, which assign relative weights to each individual piece of data in interpreting the input. The "deep" in deep learning refers to using tall stacks of these layers to collectively uncover more complex patterns in the data, expanding its understanding from pixels to basic shapes to features like stop signs and brake lights. To train the networks, programmers repeatedly test them on large sets of data, automatically tweaking the weights so the network makes fewer and fewer mistakes over time".

"While research into neural networks, is indeed loosely based on the human brain, it dates back decades, progress has been particularly remarkable in roughly the past ten years, Nicholson says. A 2006 set of papers by renowned computer scientist Geoffrey Hinton, who now divides his time between Google and the University of Toronto, helped pave the way for deep learning's rapid development."

"This year, a Google-designed computer trained by deep learning defeated one of the world's top Go players, a feat many experts of the ancient Asian board game had previously thought could be decades away. The system, called Alpha Go, learned in part by playing millions of simulated games against itself. While human chess players have long been bested by digital rivals, many experts had thought Go — which has significantly more sequences of valid moves — could be harder for computers to grasp."

"Vicente notes a group from the University of Oxford unveiled a deep learning-based lip-reading system that can outperform human experts. And this week, a team including researchers from Google published a paper in the Journal of the American Medical Association showing that deep learning could spot diabetic retinopathy roughly (almost) as well as trained ophthalmologists. That eye condition can cause blindness in people with diabetes, especially if they don't have access to testing and treatment."

"At the present stage of development there are of course limitations, but the potential is growing exponentially, day by day."

"And, the experts say, with a bit of awe, that the math operations involved aren't beyond an advanced high school student. Some clever matrix multiplications to weight the data points and a bit of calculus to refine the weights in the most efficient way are the most that is required. As it is though, at the present time, only modern computers, along with an internet-enabled research community sharing tools and data, have made deep learning practical."

"At the same time, if one steps back, the following comes to mind. "

"First, eventually these systems can become as prevalent as to make people believe that a certain action is justified (It's proven by computer, they would say). The methods could be used by persons with hidden and dangerous agenda, and the systems could encounter an error because they cannot really iterate creatively as well as humans. Finally, if a certain mode of behavior becomes universal there is the possibility that the governing machine could be "crashed" or hacked disastrously by one or more persons."

"In addition to creating artificial intelligence through neural networks, these networks are indeed, already operating in the Cybersphere. There is a direct influence they have on people day by day that it appears is becoming more universal. Does this not require ongoing analysis of evil data vs. gullibility?"

"<u>Brain Computer Interfaces:</u> More directly related to the brain and influence therein, SpaceX and Tesla are backing a brain-computer interface venture called Neuralink, according to The Wall Street Journal. The company, which is in the earliest stages of existence and has no public presence whatsoever, is centered on creating devices that can be implanted in the human brain, with the eventual purpose of helping human beings merge with software and keep pace with artificial intelligence, making humans smarter. These enhancements could improve memory or allow for more direct interfacing with computing devices. "

"The company's director told a group in Dubai, "Over time I think we will probably see a closer merger of biological intelligence and digital intelligence." He added that "it's mostly about the bandwidth, the speed of the connection between your brain and the digital version of yourself, particularly output." On Twitter, he has responded to inquiring fans about his progress on a so-called "neural lace," which is sci-fi shorthand for a brain-computer interface humans could use to improve themselves."

"This has not stopped a surge in Silicon Valley interest from tech industry futurists who are interested in accelerating the advancement of these types of far-off ideas. To be fair, the hurdles involved in developing these direct to brain devices are immense."

"Yet the attempts continue. Facebook's "direct brain interface," a creation of its secretive Building 8 division, could take tech-enhanced communication to the next level."

"In fact, Facebook has been exploring a silent speech system with a team of more than 60 scientists that would let people type 100 words per minute with their brain. What if you could type directly from your brain... with the speed and flexibility of voice and the privacy of text?" "It is noted that there are a number of computer and information specialist pointing out that such a method invites intrusion into the brain waves of participants."

"Even so, it is becoming clear that implanting in humans is not an absolute requirement, as there is are many examples where the overarching Cybersphere takes hold!"

"<u>Authorities Influence:</u> Reporter Todd of NBC news made an interesting point, one that relates directly to the matter of cyberspace influence."

"It is clear that political campaigns have become so tech-savvy (read cyber implanted and controlled) they can target the exact voters needed for a victory, often eschewing debates over critical issues, even telling lies, and ignoring sets of voters. Further redistricting with the use of finely tuned data sets, is used to protect incumbent legislators and produce further polarization. "We are sending lawmakers to govern who don't have any incentive to compromise", the reporter noted. "So voters are forced to pick a side, eliminate nuance altogether. And this leads to creating conflicts that can effect advance into reasonable governance. The notion that the other party threatens the nation, becomes a heightened relationship between people."

"Social Networking: And into this is the simple and direct way that the use of our mass communication-internetting capability is presently showing evidence of affecting the human psyche. Here we can turn to studies on the effect of our "interlinks" via social networking. There are presently a number of studies that show the pervading influence of cyberspace and certainly the interest of serious minded people in it."

"On line such as "Facebook" does give us more friends. A 2011 survey by Pew Research backs this up, suggesting people who communicate using social media and mobile phones have more close friends than those who don't. On the other hand, there are real concerns as we are just beginning to grasp the reality."

"The more people use Facebook, like posts, share their own links and are exposed to the carefully crafted profiles of their friends, the worse they will feel, a study by the John Hopkins Bloomberg School of Public Health suggests. It had already been cited as behind some serious downward effects on young people, who when cyberbullied via it, committed suicide!"

"Previous investigations into the use of social media have suggested that retreating online and away from face-to-face social relationships can lead to sedentary behavior and internet addiction. However, the more in-depth study by the John Hopkins Bloomberg School of Public Health has found that almost every form of interaction with Facebook can lead to diminished well-being."

"Writing in the Harvard Business Review, Shakya and Christakis said the three Facebook behaviors they measured to include liking, posting, and clicking links all led to negative self-comparisons and made people feel worse about themselves. They expected liking other people's content to be the largest driver of decreased happiness but said overall the sheer quantity of time people spent interacting with the social media app led to the negative effects."

"The results were particularly concerning for mental health. Most measures of Facebook use in one year predicted a decrease in mental health in a later year. This research found consistently that both liking others' content and clicking links significantly predicted a subsequent reduction in self-reported physical health, mental health, and life satisfaction," they added. The data base here was from over five thousand adults over two years. Yet, how the use of the social media caused the effect is not presently clear. However, these researchers concluded: "What seems quite clear ... is that online social interactions are no substitute for the real thing."

"A study, published by Oxford University Press, collected three sets of data from 5,208 U.S. adults over two years and measured how their mental health, reported physical health, and body-mass index changed over time relative to their use of Facebook. It also collected information on the subjects' real-world social interaction. While the numbers showed use of the social network led to a lessened sense of well-being, how exactly that happened was unclear, however."

"Ultra-easy Internet Linked Information: In addition to social networking per se, the long-term effects of technology use on the many available networks are still unknown."

"It is clear that internet linked technology information is changing the way we learn and are changing the way we think," says Dr. Benjamin Storm, Associate Professor of psychology at University of California Santa Cruz. "However, in the same way that advances in technology are outpacing our understanding of what it's doing to our behaviors and relationships, those changes are also outpacing our understanding of how it's affecting learning and thinking", says Storm, who studies human memory and cognition. In a recent study, Storm and his colleagues found that offloading one piece of information even the simple act of saving a computer file actually made it easier to learn an unrelated piece of information."

"And while rapid access technology is expanding our worldviews and social circles there are serious questions as to what the easy access may be doing to our inherent ability to think things through! Here are some thoughts on that gathered from various studies that appear here and there in magazines and the press."

"Will a baby born in 2017 ever unfold a map to determine the best driving route from New York City to a small town in Massachusetts? Will that baby memorize a phone number other than his or her own? Will they grow up to be a smarter man or woman because their mind is no longer cluttered with mundane facts and the processes technology can do for us? Psychologists and neuroscientists don't know these answers yet. But they're beginning to understand how spending every waking moment within reach of Internet-connected devices is affecting our lives." "We've never have had a technology that we use so intensively for so many different things," says Nicholas Carr, author of "The Glass Cage: How Computers Are Changing Us."

"For example we are shaking up the workforce in unexpected ways. We keep our brains in a constant state of overload, always distracted by new bits of information. It's human nature to want to take it all in because at one point in history knowing everything that was going on in the environment literally helped humans survive", Carr explains. "Now, (however) constant connection to the Internet via smartphones and laptops has changed long-established rhythms of human thinking. There used to be times when we were socializing and learning from the people and the world around us and times when we were alone with our thoughts."

"But it becomes much harder to practice the attentive types of thinking---contemplative thought, reflective thought, introspective thought", Carr says. "That means it's very hard to translate information into rich, highly connected memories that ultimately make us smart and intelligent."

"Further, Technology is changing how we empathize with others. For example, our relationship with technology affects how we communicate. But it also affects the deeper ways we interact and connect with people". This is according to Dr. Sherry Turkle, professor of the social studies of science and technology at MIT and the author of "Reclaiming Conversation". "Now we can always be heard, we never need to be alone, and we never worry about being bored thanks to the constant feeds of information. If you can't be alone with your own thoughts [ever], you can't really hear what others have to say because you need them to support your fragile sense of self. True empathy requires the capacity for solitude. Even if we think we're bored, the brain is working hard to process information we've taken in to replenish itself," Turkle explains. "Just like Carr and others are concerned that this stream of distractions prevents deep thinking, Turkle's concern is that those distractions also prevent the deep feeling that lets us connect emotionally with others!"

"We need to reclaim face-to-face conversation. One 2014 study followed 51 kids who spent five days at an outdoors camp with no phones or laptops allowed. After time away from technology, the children were better able to read facial expressions and identify the emotions of actors in videos they were shown, compared with a control group of kids who didn't attend the camp."

"Less interaction with technology allows us to focus on conversations and interactions with others instead of trying to fulfill cravings for finding new information via smartphones and other devices. We need (seriously) to reclaim face-to-face conversation, never have we needed to talk to each other and understand each other more."

"<u>Digital Overloading</u>: Further serious concern is evident in that "Digital Offloading" can in fact lead to information missed. Here are some perceptive comments. "It is true that our digital devices have become a memory partner (Storm et.al). "You can make more room for new information in your brain when you store and access other information digitally. The concern, however, is that too much digital offloading means we might miss out on the mental connections that make us more creative and intelligent", Storm explains---"and that offloading may prevent us from developing the very same sort of expertise as we would otherwise."

"Further to this problem of digital offloading is the following. A study published in "Nature Communications" found that certain parts of the brain actually switch off or become less active when drivers used GPS to navigate the streets of London compared to those who relied on memory. Indeed, research suggests that using a GPS navigation system to get to your destination "switches off" parts of the brain that would otherwise be used to simulate different routes." "When we lean on GPS, we're no longer using certain parts of our brain the way we have over millennia", says Dr. Hugo Spiers, the study's author and reader in neuroscience in the Department of Experimental Psychology at University College London. "This may not be good for us, but we can't currently tell. There are plenty of unanswered questions about how new forms of technology affect our thinking and behavior or if they harm our intelligence and creativity, Storm says, and there's a danger in deciding whether the changes are good or bad." By Vicente-"There is danger in auto-deciding."

~~~~~~

At this point Chivonn, concluded her review of Vicente's dissertation for this meeting. She did this by extracting his following comment…

"First, it is important to state that I deeply honor my fellow humans. Homo sapiens is remarkable in what they can create and it is clear that a great many cherish others. However, the basic exploration, as reviewed forgoing reveals considerable potential, not only for good but evil outcomes from our now largely cyberspace implanting- developing Global Brain!

Pointedly, the matter of cyber-influx into a "Global Brain" matters greatly, because the full record of humans is one of political and often spirit linked cruel wars, where those now could be the masters of cyberspace, and so influence as to create a wholly inhuman, homo sapiens in large numbers!

In short, data manipulation, is a facet of Cybersphere that can greatly affect progress toward the Omega point, seriously putting Teilhard's impression of the creation of ultimate incredible benevolent humans, in jeopardy!

CHAPTER 5: RISING "SAFELY" TO OMEGA

Memetics and Genetics
Omega Shields Armor
The Ideologies

At the next meeting the Professor was the first to comment. "Thank you, Chivonn, for that bridge into Vicente's work. So it is that we of the Panel are discovering before he was killed Vicente had developed his dissertation proposal well beyond just cursory background. That seems clear from that which Chivonn has reviewed for us thus far."

Before beginning to complete her review, Chivonn is reminded by Dr.Y "that a dissertation supports its claim to originality by positioning its argument both within and against prior scholarship and practices. Furthermore, a strong proposal integrates the discussion of its methods into its claims to be presenting a new or distinct approach to some material or issue." Chivonn assured the Professor that what she would continue to review, fully met such criteria, and with that she opened her note folder as she had done, reading from her report a summary of Vicente's work.

…"Thus it is in his proposal-chapter Vicente treats central notions from which saving ideas arise. He chose to call the composite of these "The Omega Shield". His working hypothesis toward that is as follows."

"1. A shield for new humans must be developed to insure that final humans reach Omega as a united Humanity.

2. This Omega Shield will develop optimally when secured within the genome, in a cy-gen--- inherited and developed in future generations.

3. That can be created by present generations who honor the growth of all children through open-minded informed nurturing."

"In defense of the need for this future reaching shield, cyberspace is now everywhere and entrenches acceptance of evil as well as good. Indeed terrible acts, such as the online beheading of hostages is patently accepted by too many. Murder while you watch refers to real Facebook events.[1]

Humanity is steeped in conflict and self-interest and unlikely to last to any of Kardashev Time lines with the aura of greatness projected by Teilhard at the Omega Point."

"It is the proposal of this dissertation that the construction of an appropriate shield to reach the Omega Point in good stead, is dependent upon allowing in our new generations a sense of objectivity significantly powerful in their genetic structure to rationally dissect aberrant anti-human influences permeating the Global Brain. For purposes of simplification, we will call that genetic structure the Cy-gene!"

"That such genetic control would develop can be seen by observing the power, indeed proof of self-replicating units of culture! The critical and philosophical term is Mimesis from which is drawn a gene parallel term the "Meme".

"Memetics is the theory of mental content based on an analogy with Darwinian evolution, originating from the popularization of Richard Dawkins' 1976 book "The Selfish Gene." Proponents describe Memetics as an approach to

1. Detailed by Kathleen Parker (appearing in her article from the Washington Post Writers Group 20 April, 2017.)

Evolutionary models. In the subject called "Mimetics" there is a foundational concept in a sense leading to evidence for a Universal Brain."

"Memetics is also notable for sidestepping the traditional concern with the truth of ideas and beliefs. Instead, it is interested in their success. That is indeed a concern!

There is via that the notion that a 'meme' is a 'virally-transmitted cultural symbol or social idea'!"

"The term "meme" derives from the Ancient Greek μιμητής (mimētḗs), meaning "imitator, pretender". The similar term "Mneme" was used in 1904, by the German evolutionary biologist Richard Semon, best known for his development of the "Engram Theory of Memory" (used in Scientology). "Mimeme" comes from a suitable Greek root, but as Semon said "I want a monosyllable that sounds a bit like "gene". I hope my classicist friends will forgive me if I abbreviate Mimeme to meme. If it is any consolation, it could alternatively be thought of as being related to "memory", or to the French word meme."

"A great many people in this modern cyberspace time, have heard the term because the majority of modern memes, fall into somewhat trivial or popular ideas. They are captioned photos that are intended to be funny, often as a way to publicly ridicule human behavior. Other memes can be videos and verbal expressions.

However, some memes have, indeed, heavier and more philosophical even dangerous content!"

"The world of memes is noteworthy for two very, very important reasons: it is a worldwide social phenomenon, and memes as has been noted can be said to behave like a mass of infectious flu and cold viruses, traveling from person to person quickly through social media.

A point of focus from this wide human 'implantation', is that the meme, may be thought of, indeed, as analogous to a gene!"

"It was conceived as a "unit of culture" (an idea, belief, pattern of behavior, etc.) which is "hosted" in the minds of one or more individuals, and which can reproduce itself, thereby jumping from mind to mind.

Thus, what would be regarded as just one individual influencing another to adopt a belief is seen as an idea-replicator reproducing itself in a new host."

"As with genetics particularly under a Dawkinsian interpretation a meme's success may be due to its contribution to the effectiveness of its host.

In his 1976 book "The Selfish Gene", the evolutionary biologist Richard Dawkins, indeed, used the term meme to describe a unit of human cultural transmission analogous to the gene, arguing that replication also happens in culture, albeit in a different sense."

"Ted Cloak had briefly outlined a similar hypothesis in 1975, which Dawkins referenced. Cultural evolution itself is a much older topic, with a history that dates back at least as far as Darwin's era. Dawkins, however, in 1976 proposed that *the meme is a unit of information residing in the brain and is the mutating replicator in human cultural evolution. It is a pattern that can influence its surroundings, that is, it has causal agency – and can propagate."*

This created great debate among sociologists, biologists, and scientists of other disciplines, because "Dawkins himself did not provide a sufficient explanation of how the replication of units of information in the brain controls human behavior and ultimately culture, since the principal topic of the book was not genetics per se." "Dawkins apparently did not intend to present a comprehensive theory of Memetics in "The Selfish Gene", rather coined the term meme in a speculative spirit. Accordingly, different researchers came to define the term "Unit of Information" in different ways."

"Another stimulus was the publication in 1991 of "Consciousness Explained" by Tufts University philosopher Daniel Dennett, which incorporated the meme concept into a theory of the mind. And, in his 1991 essay "Viruses of the Mind", Richard Dawkins used Memetics to explain the phenomenon of religious belief and the various characteristics of organized religions."

"The idea of language as a virus was introduced by William S. Burroughs as early as 1962 in his book "The Ticket That Exploded", and eight years later in "The Electronic Revolution", published in "The Job". Douglas Rushkoff explored the same concept in "Media Virus: Hidden Agendas in Popular Culture" in 1995."

"However, the foundation of Memetics in its full modern incarnation originated in 1996 with publication of two books by authors outside the academic mainstream: "Virus of the Mind: The New Science of the Meme" by former Microsoft executive turned motivational speaker and professional poker-player, Richard Brodie, and "Thought Contagion: How Belief Spreads Through Society" by Aaron Lynch, a mathematician and philosopher who worked for many years as an engineer at Fermilab. Lynch claimed to have conceived his theory totally independently of any contact with academics in the cultural evolutionary sphere, and apparently was not even aware of Dawkins' "The Selfish Gene" until his book was very close to publication."

"Around the same time as the publication of the books by Lynch and Brodie the e-journal "Journal of Memetics-

Evolutionary Models of Information Transmission" appeared on the web. It was first hosted by the "Centre for Policy Modelling" at Manchester Metropolitan University but it was later taken over by Francis Heylighen of the research institute at the Vrije Universiteit Brussel. So it was the e-journal soon became the central point for publication and debate within the nascent memeticist community. "

"In 1999, Susan Blackmore, a psychologist at the University of the West of England, published "The Meme Machine", which more fully worked out the ideas of Dennett, Lynch, and Brodie. It attempted to compare and contrast them with various approaches from the cultural evolutionary mainstream it also provided novel, and controversial, Memetics-based theories for the evolution of language and the human sense of individual selfhood. About the same time there were a number of other works and publications, e-type, newsletters and more."

"However, it was in 2005, that the Journal of Mimetic's "Evolutionary Models of Information Transmission" ceased publication and published a set of articles on the future of Memetics. There was to be a relaunch but that has not occurred! "It is, however, clear from this vast interest that the notion of implantation of ideas in people is possible through deliberate mimetic driven communication.

Thus, a lingering note is this, if the meme could be genetically engineered then so can the Planetary Brain."

"Of recent times an evolutionary model of cultural information transfer has arisen! It is based on the concept that units of information, or as might be said "memes", have an independent existence, are self-replicating, and are subject to selective evolution through environmental forces."

"Starting from a proposition put forward in the writings of Richard Dawkins, it has since turned into a new area of study, one that looks at the self-replicating units of culture. It has been proposed that just as memes have effects similar to genes, Memetics is analogous to genetics."

"It is for the sake of fairness and completeness noted that there are critics. They contend that some proponents' assertions are "untested, unsupported or incorrect." For example, Luis Benitez-Bribiesca calls it "a pseudoscientific dogma" and as factual criticism, he refers to the lack of a code script for memes, as the DNA is for genes, and to the fact that the meme mutation mechanism (i.e., an idea going from one brain to another) is too unstable (low replication accuracy and high mutation rate), which would render the evolutionary process chaotic."

"This, however, has been demonstrated (e.g. by Daniel C. Dennett, in "Darwin's Dangerous Idea") to not be the case, in fact, due to the existence of self-regulating correction mechanisms (vaguely resembling those of gene transcription) enabled by redundancy and other properties of most meme expression languages do stabilize information transfer. For example, spiritual narratives including music and dance forms can survive in full detail across any number of generations even in cultures with oral tradition only."

"Memes for which stable copying methods are available will inevitably get selected for survival more often than those which can only have unstable mutations, therefore going extinct. Notably, Benitez-Bribiesca's claim of "no code script" is also irrelevant, considering the fact that there is nothing preventing the information contents of memes from being coded, encoded, expressed, preserved or copied in all sorts of different ways throughout their life-cycles." Chivonn interjected here, that 'this latter point on coding is telling regarding a proposition in Vicente's dissertation noted later."

"The main take away from this meme history is that globally thought processes may be influenced by mimetics. A question is---could this be used in a more active or directed way. In short, there are arguments pro and com as to whether memes per se may become an imbedded aspect of human behavior. However, there are already efforts to as noted by a number of commentators to capitalize on the "transcription process".

"Research methodologies that apply Memetics go by many names: Viral marketing, cultural evolution, and the history of ideas, social analytics, and more. Many of these applications do not make reference to the literature on memes directly but are built upon the evolutionary focus of idea propagation that treats semantic units of culture as self-replicating and mutating patterns of information that are assumed to be relevant for scientific study."

"For example, the field of public relations is filled with attempts to introduce new ideas and alter social discourse. One means of doing this is to design a meme and deploy it through various media channels. One definite historic example of applied Memetics is the public relations campaign conducted in 1991 as part of the build-up to the first Gulf War in the United States."

"The application of Memetics to a difficult complex social system problem, that is Environmental Sustainability, has recently been attempted at "thwink.org". Using meme types and memetic infection in several stock and flow simulation models, Jack Harich has demonstrated interesting phenomena that are at best, and perhaps only, explained by memes."

"One of these models the so called "Dueling Loops of the Political Power place", argues that the fundamental reason corruption is the norm in politics is due to an inherent structural advantage of one feedback loop pitted against another."

"Another application of Memetics in the sustainability space is the crowd-funded "Climate Meme Project" conducted by Joe Brewer and Balasz Laszlo Karafiath in the spring of 2013. This study was based on a collection of 1000 unique text-based expressions gathered from Twitter, Facebook, and structured interviews with climate activists."

"The major finding was that the global warming meme is not effective at spreading because it causes emotional duress in the minds of people who learn about it.

Five central tensions were revealed in the discourse about climate change, each of which represents a resonance point through which dialogue can be engaged. The tensions were Harmony to Disharmony (whether or not humans are part of the natural world), Survival/Extinction (envisioning the future as either apocalyptic collapse of civilization or total extinction of the human race), Cooperation to Conflict (regarding whether or not humanity can come together to solve global problems), Momentum to Hesitation (about whether or not we are making progress at the collective scale to address climate change), and Elitism/Heretic (a general sentiment that each side of the debate considers the experts of its opposition to be untrustworthy)." Chivonn said here that "she was impressed (as Vicente) in how subtle and permeable are our conflicting balances as we face ideas."

"Francis Heylighen of the "Center Leo Apostel for Interdisciplinary Studies" has postulated what he calls "Memetic Selection Criteria". These criteria opened the way to a specialized field of applied Memetics to find out if these selection criteria could stand the test of quantitative analyses. In 2003 Klaas Chielens actually carried out these tests in a Master's thesis project on the testability of the selection criteria."

"In the book "Selfish Sounds and Linguistic Evolution", Austrian linguist Nikolaus Ritt has attempted to "operationalize memetic concepts" and use them for the explanation of long term sound changes and change conspiracies in early English. It is argued that a generalized Darwinian framework for handling cultural change can provide explanations where established, speaker centered approaches fail to do so. The book makes comparatively concrete suggestions about the possible material structure of memes, and provides empirically rich case studies."

"And Vicente points out that there are a good number of other examples of direct studies on meme locking mentality."

"Australian academic S.J. Whitty argued that project management is a memeplex with the language and stories of its practitioners at its core. This radical approach sees a project and its management as an illusion; a human construct about a collection of feelings, expectations, and sensations, which are created, fashioned, and labeled by the human brain. Whitty's approach requires project managers to consider that the reasons for using project management are not consciously driven to maximize profit, and are encouraged to consider project management as naturally occurring, self-serving, evolving process which shapes organizations for its own purpose."

"Noteworthy in meme locking examples, Swedish political scientist Mikael Sandberg argues creative innovation of information technologies in governmental and private organizations in Sweden in the 1990s from a memetic perspective."

"Concluding the Mimetics aspect of his dissertation Vicente comets, "The importance of the meme intrusion into the Global Brain by serious researchers is evidenced the simple fact that there have become a series of terms developed around the concept. Here are some of these.

Memeplex – (an abbreviation of meme-complex) is a collection or grouping of memes that have evolved into a mutually supportive or symbiotic relationship. Simply put, a meme-complex is a set of ideas that reinforce each other.

Meme-complexes are roughly analogous to the symbiotic collection of individual genes that make up the genetic codes of biological organisms. An example of a memeplex would be a religion.

To continue with terms, a Meme pool is a population of interbreeding memes. Memetic engineering is the process of deliberately creating memes, using engineering principles. Further, Memetic algorithms are an intelligent approach to evolutionary computation that attempts to emulate cultural evolution in order to solve optimization problems.

A Memotype is the actual information-content of a meme. *A Memeoid is a neologism for people who have been taken over by a meme to the extent that their own survival becomes inconsequential. And, there are certainly examples which include kamikazes, suicide bombers and cult members who commit mass suicide.*

There is also Memetic equilibrium which refers to the cultural equivalent of species biological equilibrium. It is that which humans strive for in terms of personal value with respect to cultural artefacts and ideas

In "The Electronic Revolution" William S. Burroughs writes: "the word has not been recognized as a virus because it has achieved a state of stable symbiosis with the host."

"However, that may be it is clearly apparent that programed thought transfer through mimetics has genetic replication analogies and that notion begs the question as to what could occur at the physical genetic level!"

`,,,,,,,,,,,,,,,,,,,,,,,,,,,,,,,,,,,,,,,,,,,,,,,,,,,,,,,,,,,,`

At this point Chivonn said ..."Well, panel this constitutes a targeted selection of the research and review in Vicente's dissertation. There is much more, however, at this point I will turn to presenting his central hypothesis and proposed solution."

"As to Hypothesis, Vicente recognized, and accepted that there is development of the "Global Brain" and it is a real and a most serious consideration. It is of such importance that allowing current mere happenstance transfer from the ether, the Cybersphere, even various scurrilous mimetics to create a human future accelerating and embedding tolerance for evil would be a terrible mistake!"

"As to a "Proposed Solution", Vicente argues that the successful permeation in human thinking as is clear for example with the meme---may, he submits, occur naturally over time in the genome. He emphasizes that humans have imbedded in that genome a genetic species protective, humanitarian compulsion that is in their best interest to preserve. This is found in such historical developments as democracy, in the various faiths, all of which as they began reflected ideas of humanity."

"He proposes that must be protected, i.e. the genome must be given opportunity to retain that humanitarian

impulse for it to become a "Shielding Aspect" in what inevitably will be a global "Cy-gene" operating for humans to reach the spirit of Omega as envisioned by Teilhard.

"How can that occur?" He proposes that this come about through a twostep process".

"The first, is deeper awareness of our genetic capability and related susceptibility. "

"The second step is providing future humans ideas to obtain objective and free minded rational thinking, thus providing in time with new generations opportunity for such insight to become a functional operator within the cy-gene.

That first step, that is, deeper genetic awareness is through recognizing something that has not yet been fully realized, although this has been proposed[1]."

"Simply put, there develops in each new child, in each new generation a lingering code operating between base pairs in human DNA! It has been offered that this "Starter Knowledge" is imbedded deep in the DNA and is expressed in the way the brain detects life, events, the Cosmos and reality. (Do we not see it in the rapid awareness of babies?)

Of course, this is an awesome proposal, barely touched on before. But simply considering how naturally humans come into life with great interpretive power it is impossible to ignore.

Further and critically, it is known that hominids evolve in small biochemical but significant ways.

Thus, we have now many new enzymes to protect us as new chemicals arrive, i.e. to metabolize and detoxify them."

---

1. This proposal is first in the words of the Vistavien cited in the book "The Future Navigator", ISBN: 978-0692-40588-8.

"Changes in our cellular, DNA-biology do occur, and this must happen at the electronic level in genetic chemistry."

"The fine and specific embedding in our molecular genetics is indeed real and can be found in a wide variety of examples. Here is another one, seemingly an outlier, but just to illustrate the effects on human behavior. Researchers have found a genetic mutation that, to put a comical label on it, turns people into "Martians" at least when it comes to sleep patterns. People with the mutation tend to be night owls because it keeps them on a perpetual 24 ½ hour schedule, close if you will to the Martian 24 hour, 39 minute day. Scientists reported this in "Cell' a widely respected journal.

With their body clocks always running a little longer than everybody else's, it's like having perpetual jet lag, the researchers at the Rockefeller University report. "Carriers of the mutation have longer days than the planet gives them, so they are essentially playing catch-up for their entire lives," said Alina Patke, who headed up the research effort."

"In fact it can be justifiably argued that we do begin in each new life with a "Starter Knowledge" (argued in foot note 1. above). It is proposed that implant is in the fine structure of the DNA, not just in the helix, not in the base paring per se, but in a *sub-code* of the fine chemical attractions and cross attraction and reactions within in those base pairings and supporting protein. Chemistry forms it and it takes energy (a new life) to activate it, but it lies there always, and always improving in that subtle inter-matrix exchange of electrons and energy!"

"The notion of perpetuating mind in the living is, of course, not unique and millions of people already believe in this. Examples can be found in tribal societies. The African

Yoruba for example feel they tap this energy as Orishas or in Arada, the White Voodoo rituals!

The problem is that these beliefs do not treat mechanism. However, that such thinking has percolated up into daily lives is evidence that people sense this inner instruction although it is exhibited at the level of outward feeling. And there are other examples."

"Within the newer religion of Scientology is the same recognition which is in the Arada. That is acceptance of an inner set of passed on instruction within the brain that can be tapped. Scientology incorporates tenets from a number of world religions but most prominently it includes recognition of past lives, and considers the individual to be a spiritual being of immortal nature (called a Thetan). The belief pattern involves a technique of achieving better mental health by confronting memories that are not entirely accessible to the conscious mind, mental images associated with past moments of pain. The presence of these images which they call "Engrams (referenced above)"is held to provoke irrational behavior.

Buddhists view the mind as a consciousness that reincarnates over many lifetimes and exists to seek happiness and fulfill ones karmic destiny. They believe, justifiably, that human nature is compassionate and the science of "interior reality" is ethical as discoveries imply right actions. One might say that the Buddhists "Interior Reality" is a form of benevolent Engram."

However, they are correct, in a sense, if transferred onto a species basis. Thus, the "Theology" of the Buddhist specifies the "Goal of Human Life" as happiness. Yes, but to have human life, we must preserve the future of humanity, and each person must be healthy within! They must be able to adjust their "Truth Books."

"Even so, these philosophies are recognizing the first and kind brain as well as activation of inner signals, which it is proposed are from the sub-codes described."

"Of course, this is proposing a realm for knowledge existing in chemical signals within the DNA complexes of the brain, chemical transfers that we have to study. Although the base pair is mapped, we will expose this sub-come once we have mapped all the sub-elements of the genome. We cannot just speak of a base pair sequence, we must know of the entire supporting protein matrix and the inner base to base electron transfers. It is in those environment influenced electron transfers that matter. "

To be more specific, it is in the fine structure of the environment of the DNA, not in just the helix, not in just the base pairs, but in the sub-code of the fine chemical attractions of the entire DNA-protein complex. Chemistry forms it and it takes energy to activate it! And the activated new life chemistry in turn captures coded energy from the past."

It is in this manner that Starter Knowledge grows with each new generation. And that can be made safe, given minds free to think clearly and independently of aberrant global influences. "

"Of course, that discovery will take time, but there is already historical evidence. The evidence is simply in the transition of ability from simple hominids to Homo sapiens over millions of human life times for each simple step up toward more capable, more humane-humanity.

So, when this is deeply considered it becomes clear. With the influence of the developing global meme sets, new generations are subject to new imbedded genic structure, which with the massive overriding cyberspace influence coupled with the constantly firing human brain neuronal complex---can be appropriately named Cy-genes."

"These are proposed here as not just in the ether as a global brain, but they are in fact a real physical composite of that which will develop in the hominid brain at large. And that will be, if inappropriately developed- the imbedded tragic fate of humans, or with hope the bright Omega for mankind."

"How can that intelligent, analytical Cy-gene carrying us toward the Omega Point be shielded, made in net rational?"

"The following is suggested. This is not a dictated gene implant, it is a proposed learning pathway, one to guard against universal deep repetitive aberrant anti-human inserts from the Cybersphere. These suggestions are intended as information measures for those who choose to protect the deep future of human kind. Here are those Information measures.

1.Information is provided via established science that Forever is real, a chemical physical infinite creation. Thus, whatever one makes of oneself that is what one is always and that is for everyone. This provides a moral basis for a sense of humanity.

2.Information is provided on the natural growth mechanism of children. That is, the real need for learning self-dependence toward becoming self-actuating, and free minded persons, without pre-embedding superstitious dogma.

3.Information be provided on developing a free and open, rational (centered) Mind.

4.Information be provided on the advantages of knowledge ecology management for organization, shielding against the cruel negative side for the cy-gene.

These ideas should be held ideally by those who join the ranks of a new set of voyagers, worldwide Future Navigators.

That is, the Omega Shield is the rational formation in forthcoming generations of stable self-actuating-mindful Cy-genes. These will be developed in the Genome via children with education toward critical minds as their inevitable exposure to cyberspace occurs. These are necessary due to the potential for an ever growing, aberrant Global Brain, influenced by the immense worldwide cyberspace!"

After that read through Chivonn ends up her review as follows. "Lastly, in the dissertation, Vicente includes four educations. These educations detail the importance and methods underlying achieving his "Omega Shield Humane Cy-genes".

"I have handed out copies of these Ideologies. (The reader of this book will find them beginning page 108).

So then we have Vicente's core proposition, his proposal, his defense and his solutions so far provided."

"He left a short note with his writings, attached to the cover. It read, "The subject enclosed is extraordinarily serious and important. What I decided in the end was to construct my "Shield Defenses" as a set of ideologies to "Fight Fire with Fire". I hope all will understand." *Vicente Costa*

"And, of course, he offers appropriately a conclusion as follows."

"What is needed is the development of a unified knowledge ecosystem functioning in the Cybersphere contering the untoward effects permeating that sphere. The core of that is in the benevolent foundation of faiths, and the recognition in education supported and promulgated by cores of Future Navigators that each individual is allowed to reach self-actualization with open minds based on objective humanistic foundations.

This agenda will constitute as Omega is reached an "Omega Shield" via wise meme excited genomes-that will help insure its outcome holding against the collapse of human society in a cataclysm of religio-polymics---a sad energy implosion of wasted disappearing lives ---in Forever."

With that Chivonn indicated she was finished with her review of Vicente's work and looked toward the Professor to finalize the meeting!

The Professor summarized this way. "It is, in fact in my judgement an actual completed dissertation which our new student Chivonn has been reviewing for the panel."

"I suggest, and with your approval, we have the work presented to his supervisory committee posthumously! The intention is that they will evaluate his suggestions and decide to accept or reject it as a completed dissertation, awarding him the degree posthumous and as a matter of completing the university record."

We will listen to their opinion, so as to adjust further research in our laboratory. Should his committee reject posthumous awarding of a doctorate for Vicente, we will, in honor of his life and contribution, work to have it published in a statured journal or in book form. The Forever Panel all with favorable comments unanimously agreed!

~~~~~~

Some six months later at the beginning of the summer semester, the doctoral committee deciding on Vicente' dissertation met at the request of Dr.Y. The matter was not only in respect for Vicente, but was reasoned a worthwhile academic endeavor. They, the Future Evolution Panel were brought in as posthumous representatives, where questions might arise the full Forever Panel.

At the meeting, traditional in doctoral defenses' the proposal was reviewed, but this was by Chivonn the new student standing in for Vicente, an exercise she felt quite worthwhile, clearly evident in the pride she showed when presenting.

After the meeting there were two weeks of consideration by the supervisory committee and written opinions and votes sent to the Chair who called a meeting on a Friday afternoon.

All came to the meeting with great curiosity. After coffee and general pleasant conversations the meeting was called to order and the Chair read the consolidated opinion of the committee.

"It is our unanimous opinion that we would not have approved Vicente's submission had he lived at its present stage. That is, as a fully approved science doctoral awarding submission. This is because, although the proposal is based on much factual argument, the underlying notion of an Omega Point, that is-- an end to human existence, is not universally agreed, though it is often a suspected, possibility. Succinctly, the work as submitted from a Science Laboratory to a Science Doctoral Committee is not a totally scientific work but one of philosophy and sociology in theology. Unfortunately, the candidate did not matriculate in a Theology or for that matter a Philosophy Division and in a mistake by all those faculty are not on this committee. It is of course given the complexity of the effort understandable that such omission was made.

At the same time the entire committee was convinced that this follow up on Teilhard's proposals was highly meritorious. It is an exemplary scholarly work, and it should be mentioned that a majority of the committee admitted to being convinced that we humans do indeed face an Omega Point, and if we reach that it will only be one of merit, by our societies following close to proposals, such as that of Mr. Vicente's. He is careful not to make those dictatorial, where they would not receive support, or that go wrong but to encourage cores as he called them of "Future Navigators" to insure the continuation for the sense of benevolent humanism. This in the end put aside a concern by Professor Alfred Henry that Mr. Costa was advocating forced genetic engineering.

Obviously the Future Evolution panel was disappointed, probably most so by the Professor who first advocated the research for Vicente.

However, when the meeting was adjourned, the Forever Panel continued in the meeting room and expressed each and every one that it was indeed wise and respectful to have Vicente's "Dissertation in Posthumous" brought to test under a doctoral committee.

Before the panel adjourned Chivonn was asked if she intended to further pursue the Shield in same vein as Vicente.

She said, "She would be proud to do that but that the launching idea for her dissertation was given its impetus through the notion of cyberspace inserting into the genome." That she thought she could show by science experiments, although that a great challenge.

In point, she would use the growing tools at hand to show how fine inter-base pairs interactions within DNA could create a real and operating cy-gene, the starter knowledge of newborn that given the kind of Shield advocated by Vincente would grow to insure a stellar Omega Point!

The Omega Shield
Strategic Webnet Armor

Homo sapiens evolved "Human" surviving because of their instinct genetically embedded benevolence containing a sense of intelligent humane sympathy. This has been against almost unimaginable challenges, the twisting of greed, the Religio-polimics in un-rational punishments for differences in faiths and beliefs, the lack of understanding that all people no matter color or origin are of the same birth right, human beings.

Still at the present time there remain within the warring groups, the faiths and politics, are the semblance, the cores of humanity. Meanwhile, humans have created a new overlord, via their communicating machines! This cyberspace is making into them, their thought driven processes a "Global Brain". The underlying mechanisms of that have the potential to fade away from them the very sense of humanity that has seen them this far.

It is clear that there is need for shielding to help them evaluate and adjust those challenges, for the sake of their survival.

While the various groups of faith and consideration have in their beginning agenda the means to accomplish that the evidence, the entire history is that their deflections will not allow sufficient strength challenged with the onslaught of cruel and selfish acceptance to make their peaceful future happen.

There can only be one path to navigating the distant future toward Omega. This is attention the free and strong mindedness of the young--- the coming generations. That inborn gene of benevolence requires a shield!

Following are guiding protocols, ideologies toward securing their rational---humanitarian Cy-gene development guarding against the permeation of cyberspace generated inhumanity. Proposed are The Method (The Armor), and The Ideologies' (The Armor Guards, that is Protect, Develop, and Insure.)

METHOD

It is proposed that "International Interlinking Webnets" are created connecting child oriented agencies who will disseminate a set of fundamental Ideologies throughout the cyber linked Noosphere. Their activity will prioritize response when the developing global brain becomes occluded with child damaging and misleading information.

The interlinked agencies will function via a Systematic Knowledge International Ecology System (SKIES). This knowledge ecosystem will oversee knowledge management regarding the needs and growth of children, as they may be negatively affected by Cybersphere evolutionary changes. SKIES will be constructed so as to unite groups of Future Navigators, people who believe in a secure future for the world's children.

SKIES will accomplish its mission through collaborative cyberspace networks in formal collaboration agreements. Decisions on publication and issuances will be through arbitration among the participating networks, with full disclosure to one another.

The linked organizations are charged first with insuring that Ideologies on Child Development, example as published below, are given all opportunity for priority distribution in strategic cyberspace appearances.

They are charged- in connection- to search for better more humanitarian outcomes, including new solutions, to the management of knowledge resources. This recognizes the massive acquisition of knowledge, stored and decimated in the age of the Cybersphere. They are missioned to give intelligent consideration to all "knowledge resources" of and within cyberspace!

The knowledge ecosystem shall foster the dynamic evolution of knowledge interactions between entities to improve decision-making and innovation through improved evolutionary networks of collaboration. In this pursuit they are charged to consider issuances that are less child destructive, more efficient, more fair, and responsive to human needs. They will operate according to the following mandates.

They will place emphasis on organizations who are focused on social justice, with care not to avoid the most vulnerable populations, including low-income persons and marginalized groups. This recognizes that huge hosts of people live in the margins of the global economy, and that our entire planet as the Noosphere---The Global Brain grows depends upon knowledge for economic and personal development, education and health, political power and freedom, culture and is enjoyable.

The organizational framework will undertake and publish research and new ideas, engage in global public interest advocacy, provide technical advice to governments, and firms, work to enhance transparency in policy making in those entities.

In a prime assignment they will monitor actions of key actors with attention to child growth disrupting or contaminating enterprises, and provide forums for interested persons to discuss and debate the fundamental knowledge ecology topics. Decisions regarding issues of prominence will be though a panel of all participant units in the SKIES.

They will establish within National and International Agencies---Interlinked Knowledge Networking Institutions. SKIES will link knowledge resources, databases, human experts, and artificial knowledge agents to collectively provide online knowledge to achieve anywhere anytime performance of child protective actions. The availability of knowledge on an anywhere-anytime basis should be designed to blur the line between learning and performance. Both should occur simultaneously and sometimes interchangeably. Timely operating in protection of children is to be considered essential!

The networked knowledge systems will include at all times the highest state-of-the-art facility and operation to be fully actionable in the total Cybersphere. This includes the following.

SKIES will operate on two types of technological core, one dealing with the content or substantive knowledge regarding the primary objective and the other involving computer hardware and software and telecommunications, that serve as the "procedural technology" of operations. These technologies should develop their knowledge management capabilities that in goal are far beyond individual human capacity. They should provide communications between computers and among humans permitting knowledge ecosystems to be interactive and responsive within the wider community and within all of its subsystems.

The supporting system for securing humane knowledge will include research and development experts, operational managers and administrators, software systems, archival knowledge resources and databases should be the very best that can be assimilated.

Performative actions will include persistent monitoring of the effects of Cybersphere memes on the behavior of children. This is through accepted practice in child behavior analysis. At option of medical communities, under informed consent agreements the gene status of each new generation is encouraged. That is recommended at time the internal workings, i.e. sub-codes of the Cy-gene have become known.

.

~~~~~~~~~~~~~~~~~~~~~~~~~~~~~~~~~~~~~~~

IDEOLOGIES-CORE PRINCIPLES

SKIES essential charge is the maintenance and growth of the admirable characteristics in humans, this against the degrading influences of the Cybersphere that creates the loss of their humanity, their concern and sympathy for others.

Humans have developed an initial sense of morality, redemption, empathy, and broad humanitarian sensitivity. The preservation of these preserving senses and the natural growth toward the magnificent creatures at the Omega Point the human spirit evolving magnificently, must be preserved in the genetic development of each new generation.

Underlying the preservation and optimal growth of these star reaching characteristics are three basic ideologies for universal dissemination, namely Protect, Develop and Insure.

Following are examples of primary ongoing idealities that SKIES would work to insure and extend into the future of human kind to provide the needed stable consistency

PROTECT

Irrational wars, starvation, faith-based crimes…greed against children threatens our future. Therefore, we adopt the following, a manifesto of values and behaviors. These are to unite the highest doctrines of Humankind into a "Final Code of Conduct," the system by which our children will survive in peace, happiness and productivity for all the future.

1. That there is no dogma in faith that demands converting, dominating, injuring or killing a "non-believer".
2. That philosophical, political, or national dogma used as the reason for harming any person is deception amounting to crimes against Humankind.
3. That children will not be used as monetary capital for any reason. Capital means returning love to them.
4. That murder is an act of insanity; persons committing this crime will be isolated from the population.
5. That those religious beliefs based upon the values, characteristics, and behaviors best in and for all human beings should be harbored without prejudice.
6. That every child from the first dawning of cognitive ability should be know that the whole of humanity is their family above all sects, states, or nations.
7. That every adult person will freely contribute every day an act to support planet Earth and an act contributing to the movement of the species throughout the Cosmos. From Earth's model, we will move into and find ways to reside in the broader Cosmos, to create Earth like places, "Tera-Realms".

8. That all governments will be guided as their first principle by this; anyone who denigrates, injures or kills a child commits a capital crime against the species.

9. That every government shall codify these principles in the laws of their nation.

10. We vow to the upbringing and education of all children as enumerated following.

1.) Every child will be guarded and supported to the finest health and education from birth at every place on the planet. We recognize that any child could be the seed to the "Final, Perfect Ultimate Human." So, all will be given the chance to mature in a safe and supporting environment.

2.) We will begin all our actions by never removing hope from any child! We recognize the line between hunger, and anger is a thin line. Universal education of the world's children cannot occur in a world at war. We will work exhaustively to prevent the loss of young life through starvation or in wars of idealism. Complete removal of war, will be the goal of each person on this planet.

3.) Each day we will honor the following practices born in the faiths and philosophies over the history of Humankind.

<u>Islam:</u> From the faith of Islam, we adopt the following. Children have the right to be fed, clothed, and protected until they reach adulthood. They must have the respect to enjoy love and affection from their parents. They have the right to be treated equally, in relation to their siblings in terms of financial gifts. Parents will provide adequately for children in inheritance. Children have the right to education. A saying attributed to Muhammad relates: "A father gives his child nothing better than a good education."

<u>Christianity:</u> From the Christian Faith, we adopt the following. Train a child to respect this idea "He will do unto others as he would have done to him."

<u>Judaism:</u> From the Jewish Faith, we adopt and will hold the following. Girls will be given the same level and quality of education and the same in all rights as boys.

<u>Buddhism:</u> From the teachings of the Buddha, we will hold the following. We support our children to become generous, compassionate, virtuous, responsible, skilled and self-sufficient beings. We will give them the basic mental skills they need to find true happiness. To that, the most important thing is helping them to understand that every action has consequences. Each of those actions will determine their happiness, not only in the moment, but in the future. That is the basic lesson of karma, or cause and effect.

<u>Hinduism:</u> From the Hindu belief, we consider the following. It is that one should discover and explore spirituality, religion and God on one's own, and that we shouldn't interfere. It's okay to share and teach. It's another to misuse God to strike fear in others.

<u>Pantheism:</u> If you choose to believe in a god, hold that personally without evil intent to others. Recognize that each faith's prophet would have the main message from the same God; there would be no other choice, one believing in one god. In this there is thus-no reason for a polemic. However, above all rest in the beauty of the world into which you were born, so sympathetic with your existence, in that alone is the unification of all faith. Stand unified in those ideas, the same God, the same creations, your precious earth.

<u>Atheism:</u> From the Atheist, we pay attention to the following. Early implantation of religion should avoid damaging in the following ways because children are especially vulnerable to

mental harms related to it. This includes extreme guilt about normal, healthy sexual functions, disrespect for science and reason, feeling war like toward others, which do not hold the same faith. Remember, free inquiry on all matters, strengthens the species.

Further to Protection of Children:

We will help children along the path to self-control. This means they grasp reality, the karma of their lives. That means to understand things as they really are and to realize the truths of life, to see things through, to grasp the impermanent and imperfect nature of worldly objects and ideas. Since our view of the world forms our thoughts and our actions, this view, developing self-control, yields right thoughts and actions for all people.

Children will guarded such that they grow in to self-actuation. For them will be available to discover be educated with a higher sense of purpose, the realization the Cosmos is for our species a provided ideology because they are first Cosmos-lings! As they view this future, we will help them to understand that Earth is their glorious ark. It must last for thousands of generations. In its beauty, in the naturalness of earth's sympathy for our species, we have been matured. An ideal it would be that, even if most are elsewhere, this beautiful so precious home would exist as it has been found until it dies as it must through Space-time forces against which there is no possible reversal.

Children will be informed as to the matter of how our species is improving. We have become aware that of all the species, our strongest suit is our ever maturing brain. Our species agenda is to continue that remarkable development.

This means that their Brain DNA in transferring and improving through the living generations insures the arrival of "Ultimate Humans." The young will be provided insight into this so that they may respect it as adults.

We will teach our children to join in the mission of feeding all the world population. Sapiens can mobilize to go to the moon that same species can certainly mobilize the fair feeding of the world's children, in every corner. The young should have full insight into this as the charge of all humans when adult!

Children will be informed about the conflicting forces that create behavior. The brain driven urge to destroy is an embedded part of the survival of the fittest, yet that drive refers to the physical and with self-control can be managed. The brain driven urge of benevolence is also embedded. It is that drive that referees the preservation of the species. It is our strongest suit, the ability to think things through. The young should have full insight into this as a principle to reflect upon when adult.

Children will be allowed and guided by example into ethical and mental self-improvement. That is, resistance to the pull of desire, resistance to feelings of anger and aversion, and not to think or act cruelly, violently, or aggressively, and to develop compassion. This education will avoid proselytizing children into beliefs for which there is no substantiation.

We will teach the young that their children will be the next form of their species, the path to the future and full enlightenment. This means that as adults, they will take responsibility for their reproduction. Wise and considerate human pairs will inevitably begat wiser ones. To aid children of each new generation adults will be provided an understanding of how natural development can lead to their children becoming self-activating, naturally transcending, humans. If humans could do this we benefit, female and male interaction would be equal without female victimization by men.

DEVELOP

The buffer and the guide to develop healthy-minded humans in each generation is to respect that they have psychology of needs. Respect for this development in face of damaging cyberspace influences will produce more secure, self-actuation persons. The human mind is complex and different motivations can occur variously in different lifetimes. They can be arrayed, however, much as in a pyramid, although each person from their starter knowledge may experience these differently, some in sequence others some aspects may occur simultaneously. None-the-less the fundamental transition in growth to adult to be respected is as follows. SKIES activities will attend to insuring that these are published so as to be recognized and fortified.

Physiological needs

Physiological needs are the physical requirements for human survival. If these requirements are not met, the human body cannot function properly and will ultimately fail. Physiological needs are crucially important; they should be met first. Air, water, and food are metabolic requirements for survival in all animals, including humans. Clothing and shelter provide necessary protection from the elements. *As noted a prime agenda of SKIES to make aware when societies are being denied this fundamental due to cyberspace interference in needed relevant communication.*

Safety needs

Once a person's physiological needs are relatively satisfied, their safety needs take precedence and dominate behavior. In the absence of physical safety – due to war, natural disaster, family violence, childhood abuse, etc., people may re-experience post-traumatic stress disorder or transgenerational trauma. In the absence of economic safety due to economic crisis and lack of work opportunities these safety needs manifest themselves in ways such as a preference for job security, grievance procedures for protecting the individual from unilateral authority, savings accounts, insurance policies, disability accommodations, etc. This level is more likely to be found in children as they generally have a greater need to feel safe.

Safety and Security needs include, Personal security, financial security, Health and well-being, And a Safety net against accidents/illness their adverse impacts. *SKIES can help here by insuring that false promises (scamming) are on notification.*

Love and belonging

After physiological and safety needs are fulfilled, the third level of human needs is interpersonal and involves feelings of belongingness. This need is especially strong in childhood and it can override the need for safety as witnessed in children who cling to abusive parents. Deficiencies within this level due to hospitalism, neglect, shunning, ostracism, etc. can adversely affect the individual's ability to form and maintain emotionally significant relationships in general, such as Friendships, Intimacy, and Family.

Humans need to feel a sense of belonging and acceptance among their social groups, regardless whether these groups are large or small. For example, some large social groups may include clubs, co-workers, religious groups, professional organizations, sports teams, and gangs. Some examples of small social connections include family members, intimate partners, mentors, colleagues, and confidants.

Humans need to love and be loved by others. Many people become susceptible to loneliness, social anxiety, and clinical depression in the absence of this love or belonging element. This need for belonging may overcome the physiological and security needs, depending on the strength of the peer pressure.

Inherent in this is the social grouping that arises from cyberspace. Where that is obviously dangerous, example, suicide groups, or such as terrorist organizations, SKIES should provide warnings and options to bring individuals back to rational need-standings.

Esteem

All humans have a need to feel respected; this includes the need to have self-esteem and self-respect. Esteem presents the typical human desire to be accepted and valued by others. People often engage in a profession or hobby to gain recognition. These activities give the person a sense of contribution or value. Low self-esteem or an inferiority complex may result from imbalances during this level in the hierarchy. People with low self-esteem often need respect from others; they may feel the need to seek fame or glory. However, fame or glory will not help the person to build their self-esteem until they accept who they are internally.

Psychological imbalances such as depression can hinder the person from obtaining a higher level of self-esteem or self-respect. Most people have a need for stable self-respect and self-esteem. The psychologist Maslow noted two versions of esteem needs: a "lower" version and a "higher" version.

The "lower" version of esteem is the need for respect from others. This may include a need for status, recognition, fame, prestige, and attention.

The "higher" version manifests itself as the need for self-respect. For example, a person may have a need for strength, competence, mastery, self-confidence, independence, and freedom. This "higher" version takes precedence over the "lower" version because it relies on an inner competence established through experience. Deprivation of these needs could result in an inferiority complex, weakness, and helplessness.

Caution should be issued by SKIES where the influx of cyber enterprises tends to lower self-esteem, and conversely, applications into cyberspace that help persons to see their value are exercises well within SKIES agenda.

Self-actualization

"What a person can be, they must be." This quotation forms the basis of the perceived need for self-actualization. This level of need refers to what a person's full potential is and the realization of that potential. This this level is expressed as the desire to accomplish everything that one can, to become the most that one can be. Individuals may perceive or focus on this need very specifically. For example, one individual may have the strong desire to become an ideal parent. In another, the desire may be expressed athletically. For others, it may be expressed in paintings, pictures, or inventions. *To **understand** this level of need, the person must not only achieve the previous needs, but master them. Protection of that capability against degradation of it from Noosphere influences is clearly a priority of SKIES.*

Self-transcendence

The above staging in life were set down originally by A.H Maslow, who wrote on "The Hierarchy of Needs". Maslow explored a further dimension of needs. The self only finds its actualization in giving itself to some higher goal outside oneself, in altruism and spirituality. *This involves Transcendence, a state that is a critical agenda applying to the Global Brain for SKIES in its overseer role, as protection of this state is fundamental to the advance of humans---optimally arising toward the Omega Point. "Transcendence refers to the very highest and most inclusive or holistic levels of human consciousness, behaving and relating, as ends rather than means, to oneself, to significant others, to human beings in general, to other species, to nature, and to the cosmos".*

If healthy, and the path can be supported, growing children will be prepared at some point in their lives to "Self-Actualize", and from there to explore the minds-eye, seeking, stability and independence of thought. Children in that state express empathy. So released, they are easily recognized, and are set to interpret the way to reach their own goals at first on their own, and in that contribute to societies, benevolent and strong growth. *That is SKIES will serve as one means to protect this growth potential and through this create opportunity for people to develop clear headedness, in open and capable analytic minds. The path to that protected by*

SKIES is one of capping or insurance, and is enumerated following.

INSURE

Open mindedness is an essential to maintain the sense of humanity that will derive from the child protective and growth development programs. Via this means the protected, matured individual will resist the aberrant influences in cyberspace. From parent to child over generations the idealized will bring the Noosphere into a star reaching Nirvana. Here are steps in mind development to be preserved for individuals (and addressed to them) to help in that growth.

1. Understand Chaos. We live with a sense of Chaos, but if it comes to ordering, if mental calm occurs - patterns can become aware and confusion can be employed to move creativity. New thoughts are generated. We can gain clearer light. Following helps in removing the sense of Chaos.

2. Know Dream Reality From Possible Reality. There is an edge to reality. We are often unable to grasp it clearly. It is as if truth exists over a razor's edge. Thus, we live in the dream of immortality. Be calm, realize it, there is the reverse side to everything and know that even the reverse has a reverse-these, we may never be able to see. So then you are back to the only possible reality for you day to day, the present you! *Your Mind it is that which governs your reality!*

3. Respect The Cosmos. Remember, the Cosmos and our world is older than us. We are the end of a long chain of response, whatever we do the Cosmos has a head start! Reality proceeds, yet the direction we (you) set may be a part of that! If you try, and try again and fail, the Cosmos is

speaking to you. If you feel success, you are in the possible process!

4. <u>In Thinking Gain Freedom.</u> Freedom and Security are interdependent, yet by separating them in our minds we grow. Security has a definite small connotation. Freedom has a large and unlimited connotation. Behind Security, there are boundaries, when we are able to cut through them there is Freedom. Freedom from boundaries puts one within an understanding of how their lives fit within the Cosmos. The mind cannot expand unless the center is preserved. That is achieved by selecting wise boundaries. With incomplete or arbitrary boundaries the whole structure endangers collapse. A wise center allows for delightful freedom. (Protecting the center of one's mind; makes it a capable mind, then the future has potential to be protected.)

5. <u>Protect Your Mind.</u> The preciousness of your mind is impossible to underestimate. Use it or be abused by it!

6. <u>Make A Capable Mind.</u> The cause is given meaning by your noting the effect carefully! Know then that a single event is a tunnel through which all events reflect. These two--cause-effect-- cannot be separated. So you learn to understand them, first in the minuscule which leads one to understand the macro that is the most important. In bees, it is the multifaceted eye...in humans it is your capable mind that can see that you see!

7. <u>Overcome Interrupted Mind.</u> The mind is full of noise, contributing to that sense of Chaos. Focus until it quiets to a single sound! Then will occur but one voice. Silence, frees one from interfering internal dialog!

8. <u>Overcome Troubled Mind.</u> Some have developed a library in their head that becomes but one book, in their view the "Truth Book." The one book mind attempts to avoid

becoming contaminated by outside ideas. This is a system with such strong boundaries that it leads to defending self, then to bigotry and wars!

9. <u>Realize The Difference Between Belief And Freedom.</u> Belief takes meaning into formalization, then fossilization. However, if understanding is allowed to shift, each moment can be a path to freedom.

10. <u>Believe Just First In Everything.</u> Much of conflict between people is from colliding beliefs. So, practice believing initially in everything! Yes, that sounds strange, but internally, in time, the parts will sort logically, leading to one giant idea, hence, no boundaries! This should free one from the desire to be always right (which most of us have). Great problems can be solved, sometimes by evaluating the wrong. One should rather be happier in ideas that can be improved, than fearing the wrong.

11. <u>Allow Time To Grow</u>. Focus on nature, it has much to say. Remember the message in the seeds. Your time will come and with it a time to grow!

12. <u>Understand Difference Between Fear And Courage.</u> Fear is controllable. In fact, if you think about it we only fear what we "see" in the future. The rest is anticipation. In fear, we begin to imagine what we can't do, rather than what we can. Dwelling on what you can't do leads to fear, dwelling on what you can do leads to courage!

13. <u>Know Change And Learning Are Interlocked.</u> To learn is to change, to change is to learn. There is no learning without change! To remain unchanged is to remain forever without comprehension.

14. <u>Understand Perception In Relation To Reality</u>. We must accept that there are both perception and reality. In fact, more aptly put, more relevant to us as persons, human life is

"Attending." We can't turn it off. It is always pointing at something…as long as we are feeling we "Attend".

15. <u>Recognize The Modes Of Attention.</u> Within our attending, there are four modes: External and Internal, Narrow and Wide. We exist or see an existence in one or the other. Learn to know the whole! When looking down also look up, expand the narrow to the wide and vice versa. Your choices at any time depend on the extent you see!

16. <u>Expand Attention To Its Twelve States.</u> Contract and magnify as you observe, use your attention! To add sparkle to the world practice alternate meditation, knowing each mode well at first. That is, recognize deeply that there are 12 states of attention: three senses; sight, hearing, touch and four modes; internal, external, wide and narrow to achieve 3x4 states. In your Mind gain, switch from external to internal using each. This will help your mind to become richer, more mature!

17. <u>Know The Basis Of Behavior And Perception</u>. We don't disagree over what we perceive (usually). We often disagree over what those perceptions mean to us individually! Thus, the behavior may be the person, how we respond gives the behavior meaning. The response is a secondary feeling, an emotion! The original perception is the primary or internal feeling. *To un-bias yourself, change variously your sense of the perception.*

18. <u>Balance Change and Response.</u> Responding to the messages of change can create meanings, thus giving you choices, access to different worlds. Changing response lets one see the world as the opportunity! This is what we call an "Open Mind".

19. <u>Enhance Attentions.</u> Practice each so it grows, make perceptions big enough to evaluate, then the distance will

lend to improved attention, enhancement and greater value. In effect, become a "Mind Tracer."

20. Learn Translation. Learn to "Translate" each state. Make light have feeling, rock have fragrance. Intelligence is limited by the number of states one cannot master in this way. The more this can be achieved, the richer is the life experience. This helps to join one in existence within the Cosmos. In unhappy situations, one shifts attention through this means, to relieve pain or boredom.

21. Move External to Internal. A skilled Mind Tracer shift's attention, external to internal to achieve their skill. They see an external and envisions its meaning internally. This means appreciating the mental processes of which there are two; "Defining" and "Exploring." Too much defining leads to narrow judgment and views, but it can be useful if balanced as it may lead to more fruitful exploration. If one starts out with the basis of looking for something, they may find something even more interesting. Pioneering something in this way for a group means the pioneer may gain a special freedom, a special feeling of accomplishment!

22. Know Type of Questioning Relates To Happiness. The essence of the Human is to understand, to be attentive. So the way in which questions are asked is important. When we question, we should use the 12 states to enjoy, this to wander, this to let the ordinary become extraordinary. Even so, the words used are quite important. "Why" is a question of dogma, leading to more Whys? "Why" questions, sometimes work, but don't necessarily lead to information particularly useful, because this is thinking virtually, totally about meaning. "How" questions are those with a more often useful basis. One is thinking about actions. "How" leads us to use our senses probing into time, space, weight. We see the

Cosmos as phenomena, take advantage of the universe's action on itself to accomplish! Our essence our mind turns wishes into use. We are excited about this skill. The skill at this is the measure of your life. It's very much about "How"!

23. Grasp Importance Of Context In Thinking. "Content," "Reality" and "Timing" only have meaning within the "Context" that they belong. They are subordinate to Context. Therefore, our ideas about them are changeable. That is these should be viewed within their specific diversity to allow one to arrive at an accurate understanding of them. We should want first to understand that process, even though in the end the outcomes become what are desired.

24. Understand The Basis Of Feelings. Feelings prompt a "Human Fog." There are two parts. Primary feelings are those of warmth, pain, satisfaction, the actual world. Secondary thoughts are the emotions and responses, the meanings we apply. They are how we think about the world. These can be and are most often mistaken, intermixed. Feelings mixing with emotions, can lead one astray. We must evaluate whether information is appropriate between the two…knowing the difference leads to better decisions.

25. Calculate Connections. Dreaming or envisioning is not a place, but a process of calculating connections between points. The insight comprehensively gained is in using the twelve states.

26. Recognize and Use Space in Mind. The mind has the property of space. Space is not just something to fill casually. In reality, within in it matter can be created from energy. Space can be thicker or thinner depending on how much has gone to matter. So Mind space has tremendous energy and promise. *Mind when stretched to a new dimension is never the same; it is now accepting new matter (ideas recorded).*

To accept something new one must "empty some mind space," then open the door and let the future in, endless possibilities can come from this.

27. <u>Avoid Depression, Madness, And Lost States.</u> This is when one has lost the RANGE of attention, i.e. the twelve states. They are not out of Mind but lost in a limited realm within it. Perceptions are fixed! The mind is safest...not locked in, but when one is exploring freely within it. To discover and reveal hidden inner riches is the most exhilarating work of all!

28. <u>Realize Differences: Religion Vs. Science and Self.</u> Religion can deflect one's attention inward in a virtue versus failure appearance to God, i.e. one is to behave in a certain way making them hostages in a sense. Science directs one's attention outward. One becomes an aggressor for making change. In a sense, both fail to strengthen the individual as they abandon "Self-Regulation". One to be happy self regulates oneself, mind, body, and spirit. Once internally sound, one can then go out to see if that changes perception. Without self-regulation, peace can only happen in a perfect world, and must fail. Anything mind can't seem to affect must be external. Oscillate between the external ideas in relation to your foundation of internal strength!

29. <u>Know The Promise Of Human Maturity.</u> "When one resides within a correctly dimensioned drum, the sound of a beating heart is greatly magnified"... "When one truly sees the magnificence of human possibility, the sound of future beating hearts amplifies one's own! " Human kind has awesome potential, but only if it continues to exist.

30. <u>Seek Aging Well.</u> The body sends strong messages to the old. To respond with courage recognize time is the one resource you have. Manage it well. Here, the most important

thing is your own voice. Learn that even now so what you say is heard. Complete is each day doing! Incomplete is unfolding! Blend these and the beauty of life unfolds. I am. Am I? Complete, Incomplete. With time ahead you are incomplete!

31. <u>Guide Yourself Internally.</u> Wanting to be perfect begins with self-control, internally. We think of the past as influencing what we should or should not do. Talking to yourself in the right way can ease the stresses produced by this. You have "Mind Police" built up in your raising and experience. These are what others want you to do, but you take control by your personal voice. Remember to change the "You" voice to the "I" voice. Internal You - leads you to some statement about yourself, usually in a bad way. "I "- needs to never tag negatively. With "I" you can change to the positive such as "I want to share my success". Cease wanting to be perfect by the demands of the Mind Police, give that up and stay with the good myth about yourself. That way, you avoid living in "a Police State." Relief is then gained. Delight is felt when your own internal voice wins.

32. <u>Change Yourself Upward</u>. With each heartbeat, we are changing. Time is the master. All our "Life Waves" are sums of our simple waves, compiling (tangled rubber strings by simile, Item 43). So how do we best change ourselves, take control of the waves? Emphasize the "I" voice, drop the you "always will be". That is with the "I" voice you gain, in effect, you control time. The "You" voice plants you in the past. Ignore it, emphasize the wonderful. The "I" voice directs you to your future. Mood is set by who is talking in your head. Be free of your past, the Mind Policing, it only continues to affect you.

33. <u>Expand The Right "Mind Code."</u> Pronouns (as above) are the way the Mind addresses itself. However, look at Mind as a verb it is what the brain does! The brain's memory is in Chaos and brain itself is a combination lock for everything. These things can be brought up in several ways; one word will evoke several meanings. Being dumb is allowing just one door to open from the Chaos! Being smart is allowing multiple doors to open. Make a Mind Code for something important to you, anything stored or just hanging there, then bring it back and expand it. Once a bit of the Chaos is trapped (put in order) let it gather new thoughts!

34. <u>Know Limits In Existence.</u> Your life exists only in your Mind! If your view of what the world is fixed, (such as what is the perfect religion, the perfect car, move, etc.) unhappiness is sure to follow. View the world as incomplete, with room to finish it. Knowing your Mind leads to knowing your body. This gives the marvel of reducing illnesses that limit you.

35. <u>Know What Is Complete And What Not.</u> For strong viewed people the world is fixed, so every discussion is a fight or an attack. If thoughts are reopened to discussion, the world is open to many things. By knowing not to complete, minds are changeable. Each can make this discovery, and a wonderful world results. Remember "It depends, also depends." We search for new places, when we have "transformed eyes."

36. <u>Solve Problems And Issues</u>. The approach to every problem, no matter how big or small can be mastered by an expansive process in your Minds-Eye. First take the problem and expand it to as large a field as you can, organizing it into a single picture in your Mind. Then rise above that picture to look down on it, and *organize* the pieces. Now the clearer

picture can be made smaller and lower it toward you. When enough small, insignificant actions become coordinated beauty and might are created! That is, the random neural discharges of brain must be linked and combined before the magic of thought, and understanding appears!

37. <u>Apply Superior Meaning.</u> Wrongly, values and beliefs become the lens through which we look, and color the way we see the world. This turns the infinite into the finite! Rather, see the world as incomplete and possible. Practice finding several meanings to each situation. The "this and that" events should not yet have true meaning. First see without seeing "Meaning"; attempt to see what actually is! Once, the big pictures are manageable stay with that optimal, adjusting slightly as you go as needed.

38. <u>See Together The World From Your Mind.</u> Nothing is completed in the world unless it is completed first in your mind. Once mastered, know what you can do and don't know what you can't do! There is no time when self-reliance wouldn't be an asset. But, seek people you can complement while avoiding those you are weaker with. At the beginning, these "Seeking's" may be muddy waters, but even muddy waters can quench a fire!

39. <u>Draw Opinions From Different Views.</u> The Mind operates differently among different peoples. Thus, the far northern people see the top and bottom of things (sun apparently rising and falling, only). The equatorial see the left and right side of things (Sun apparently rotating east to west). Remember that while we see much the same (it is the same sun), there are differences in the WAY various minds see the world. Draw opinions from different views to gain your own strength!

40. <u>Recognize You Can Change Ideas or Concepts.</u> Your Mind is extraordinary powerful. One can use it to help oneself to change the feelings about almost anything, from pain to aberrant notions. There are two ways of remembering 1.) "As it happened to you," and 2.) "As you see it happening removed from you." When it is "attached" you feel it "Here"! When detached you are at a distance from the pain or idea. If you run it backwards from that distance, you can find ways to control it until you get to the attached, so that can be rationally evaluated.

41. <u>Change Limits to Perfections.</u> The Mind can do anything through imagination; you can even envision greater imagination. In that state, you have the model! Knowing it well and with a method, what you can do is unlimited. Many institutions will not accept the unlimited. They think it is dangerous and set boundary places in children. However, humans are born to fight over limits. The space in your mind can determine what the world will be like. It is born in you. One always wants to be right, sometimes making one confused…remember through the newly activated space in your mind…more perfect things can be made out of air!

42. <u>Seek The Unknown.</u> Behind most everything there is the reverse, or the hidden, beyond your immediate vision. (Below the plant are the roots). It is also an energy that can be seen sometimes, worth the effort when one develops deep inner vision. It can give you power for an exceptional journey. Ask! Use your imagination that is the tie-in to the power. What you can compute may not seem achievable, but you know in your heart you can do it!

43. <u>Understand Time Truths.</u> Life can be compared to a rubber string, lengthening in time, along the way tangling, tangles representing trials, successes, and progeny making

again more tangles. Then when fully taught the life string let's go, snapping, releasing energy, to return to the original state, and the energy is provided to one following. (Matter will by us, neither be created nor destroyed, only return to energy. This is the natural phenomena.) You have though control of the tangles, the balance that creates or destroys them. So to do your best in life, recognize and balance destinations.

44. <u>Be Wise in Destination Choices.</u> The best lived lives see and understand destinations clearly. Choosing destinations involves two activities, 1.) Comparing, 2.) Contrasting. These are 1.) What someone wants you to do, choosing it or me, as for example in religion, or 2?) What you want to do. Comparing is using value differences, Contrasting is using exact measurement, no value implied. In Contrasting judgment is made considering things as parts, without meaning. Comparing is "the difference between it and me", contrasting is "the difference between it and It". If there is much emotion one is comparing, if not one is contrasting. As destinations are sought one asks, what is the meaning in knowing this (compare), or what is the difference between these options (contrast)? One's delight is the measure of whether they are in proportion with these two, whether they are centered rationally within their Minds-Eye! That means also one strives for simplicity in life not determined by imitation of others.

45. <u>Find Your Center.</u> Analyzing "Space" filled with objects, the objects seem to become uneven, but, there is a center to a flowing river, we can compute it but never really see it. One's Mind is full of boundaries, but there is a center. If one understands the ideas herein, one can find one's center.

At the center is a surprise – a source of happiness, a sense of rest!

46. <u>Understand Feelings</u>. Each of us has primary and secondary feelings. Moods are secondary feelings, which are either attached or hanging detached. These feelings are similar to our two nervous systems, i.e., voluntary, involuntary. For example, we see a mountain. It is fixed, high with color, angles, and dark canyons. This is the "Content Code," the involuntary. It is there. The way we see it is voluntary. This is the "Mood Code." These two give our thoughts "Meaning." If we are afraid of height, we may see an ominous fearful structure. If we have a different Mood Code, we may see the beautiful purple in the evening light on the mountains. That is the Mood Code can be different than ominous, it can be changed so can the memory of things.

47. <u>Understand How To Use "Meaning."</u> From feelings, we develop "Meanings" to events and things. All meanings are arbitrary, one's interpretation. The meaning of anything is the way we represent it in our Minds. Meaning has the power to connect Mind and Body. For example, emotions (meanings) can be registered and affect our bodies. If one changes the meaning ascribed (example, it's a lousy world), that will change how one feels. Changing another's meaning could change the world!

Meanings are guided by the constraints of our history, often making things difficult. However, if we change the meaning toward the obvious in front of us (finding order out of chaos) all else can be automatic. The obvious is the law, for which there are real consequences (what you do now can affect what happens to you in the future). If using "You" the "and" says you are damaged, then you are a different person, a damaged one. Conversely, if "I" is used you can change your perception of yourself, and become un-damaged. If one connects the two halves of the brain (the obvious to the consequences) there is enjoyment in understanding direction, a sense of delight happens!

48. <u>Recognize The Flavor Of Reality.</u> Although we have mood and content codes, we may have different moods, depending on what content we see or know. So, we can change the character of reality, how we feel in relation to it in spite of the Cosmic cause and effect. This is because the World itself has no meaning without thought we give it that through the state of our Mood Code.

Part of how we see reality is entwined with "Anticipation." If we anticipate a loss, then we are in a state of anxiety. If we anticipate a gain, we are in a state of excitement. However, knowing that moods are coded it is difficult to complain. One needs to imagine how they would code to feel in an "Up Mood."

This is not to say the world is just "Made Up." Because we have limits, we can't argue the reality per se, but we can adjust our thoughts to the "Flavor or Reality," that we choose to live with. One's life can be sour or sweet. It is a decision each can make in spite of the fixed cosmic cause and effect, within one's mind, through how they reflect on the world - change in their life can occur.

People and institutions set themselves up to define the "Flavor of Life" and expect you to agree that is the way the world is. However, there is never a totally correct answer you can live in a world you believe is right. Although there are Cause and Effect "How" you deal with it is your choice!

49. <u>Become A Decider.</u> In every journey one hopes to reach toward the end. This discourse you studied (this was a "Means" journey) now approaches that point. The last

concerns the question of becoming a Navigator, one helping others.

More than doer's maturity leads one to become a decider, making the Mind aligned and clear as outlined, then doing becomes automatic and we and the World are acting together. The mysterious is more knowable through the obvious, and we gain control of our Minds. On the other hand, the aimless path consumes.

50. <u>Navigating Others into the Future.</u> Minds gained through the "Means Journey" just taken, can heal oneself and indeed, the world. Some last valuable recognitions, sign posts with clear lettering, help toward cementing that goal.

What is needed so that one can, (internal skills gained) externalize to be of value to others---the human species? It first is important, that each person heals self, and then they can try, and will likely want to contribute in healing the world, as our humanity is built in, an inherent instinct!

The following aspects' center upon that possibility. They are as follows, A.) Controlling the Structure of our Memory (how the past affects each one of us), B.) Controlling Time, C.) Understanding the Intersection of Imagination versus Reality, D.) Asking Fruitful Questions about Your Life, and a most important thought E.) Discovering that a Mature Mind makes you a Navigator.

A.) <u>Controlling the Structure of Memory</u>. On the way to a healthy mind, one wishes to forget "bad and frightening" experience, and certainly space for wisdom is needed in our often too crowded Minds. Some of the past, of course amounts to lessons of progress, and is retained in respect. Forgetting the unacceptable, the wrong, the cruel, the selfish, though takes effort, but we have direct control over how it affects us, because as we have learned we have control over the structure of memory. So, being enlightened, we know, for example, fear can now be seen as arbitrary-an internal event, the internal component can be controlled. Fixed, Mind Books, can be re-written.

Control over memory means developing a simple set of priorities. *These priorities tell us, in a nutshell, that we first mind our own business*! We are capable of doing this when we are prepared to supervise our own instruction, without the usual boundaries! One only needs to set as priorities; self-determination, i.e. creating their own future, avoidance of trends-that gives us quilt in the end, Integrity--thus not regretting our actions, and control of the central core, i.e. the "Foundation of Self," that is, unrestricted by useless boundaries.

B. <u>Controlling Time.</u> Being attentive creatures, or ones desiring to lead, the "Future" has a significant meaning, and in fact, offers pressure in our daily lives. "Future" might be described as the consequence of present circumstances, making it in a sense static or limited. That is, to us, there are only two ideas of time. These notions are "ongoing" and "finished" which seem to "leap frog" forever. They proceed and direct all our actions in a limiting game. However, we have control by stepping back and simply asking, "What is ongoing? What is finished? We have the power to decide to turn these into "Now is Dynamic," "Then is Static." The future is, thus, opened up to more possibilities. We select successful past ideas and continue to explore. We use our available tools to regulate thought about time, recognizing that to know one thing is to open the potential to know a thousand, if not today, then tomorrow. Well-practiced ability expects success with developing ability.

C. Controlling Intersection between Imagination and Reality. This comes about when one grasps meaningful meaning. In reality, the world will do in time what it wants. Give the world the chance it will resolve everything good or bad. One then recognizes that the World sits between ones "to be" and "to do." Our lives are within i.e. between those "Spaces." In that is the important intersection, it is the one between imagination and reality! If you control yourself, then you control this environment. If one does not intersect, that is try to control this, they become impoverished.

This says in seeming paradox, but in truth one must first become self-centered in minding one's own business--- controlling one's own internal environment to achieve a really healthy and mature state! If that were achieved, for each of us, there would be no reasons for conquest, conflict or greed. We would all be safe in independence from each other, but by the same token, available as a success for each other.

D. Working toward Answers for Central Questions about Life. One last thought lingers before one rises to the Navigator State.

Each of us has most important questions guiding one's life (yes you do if you think about it, although you may not yet have addressed it). When one achieves rational answers, one becomes finally "Mentally Mature" if that answer yields happiness! The way in which this question is asked, though, is almost as important as its content. Otherwise, your "Life's Questions" can go a long way to making you quite dissatisfied. If the answer somehow defines who you are or your present state of being you are dug in and potentially sunk. For example, if you ask, "Will this last for me," you are headed into a yes or no situation that cannot succeed. Nothing here on earth lasts forever!

Here following are some thoughts that will clarify this all-important matter and put you on the way to happiness and maturity.

Eliminate yes or no answers!

(1.) Change the verb tense and the interrogative. For example, it is not "How will I obtain what I want, but how did I obtain what I wanted? The latter then leads you to open your future, from success.

(2.) When your question refers to yourself in relation to others, reverse it. For example, it is not "When will they like me,' rather, "When will I like them"?

(3.) Leave out the specific person and avoid leading the question with "Why or Where" as these lead to the need for extensive context development. (Remember "Why" takes one into a world of dogma, etc., and removes you from yourself.)

So, if the questions are done right you will ask overall "What in this situation loves me and them?" If the questions done this way work well for you, they will fill you with delight! They will direct you to the "Something" you are looking for. They will become a self-correcting life map, and that will be work done without effort because work done in a pattern of joy is work without effort.

E. Discovering that a Mature Mind makes you a Navigator. Navigation takes courage, the self-confidence, the ability to imagine, and to remain fearless, control over the Mind's apparent limitations.

Those capable of rising to this level are "Advanced Immigrants on planet earth", in a sense Navigators who avoid the errors accumulated from the past and work toward the future for all people, uninhibited with superstition.

Among them are the many who have given us the joys of life, the tools to make it work. We will call them "Vistavien"; they are exceptionally capable navigators because they know themselves in a healthy way.

~~~~~~

The ideas in this document, you have just read, have described the way to join this new bred a Vistavien-a Future Navigator.

Now you know the path. These Immigrants are those who first respect then exceed the boundaries of Mind!

After all the paradox of reality is that no image is as compelling as the one that exists in the minds-eye...When that image is vast enough, open enough, the question of belonging is finally settled; one belongs everywhere, is, strong, satisfied, productive, a true companion.one, indeed, for everyone else!

Think of the awesome potential should the whole of humanity rise to that level as time unfolds and the Noosphere encloses to yield Omega.

THE HUMAN TIME CAPSULE
AN ACCOUNTING

(Reproduced from the Book "Future Navigators on the Edge of Forever".)

We want to think of us, each---as Forever. That is a natural instinct. And, Human Time could be Forever, if we surround ourselves with an aura of wise mentality. Indeed, there are hypothetical pathways and even scientific evidence that it could be. That will not be entirely on our terms, but functions of reality within cosmic forces. So it is up to us to find ways to understand it, to live well within in it.

Given that maturity, we do have the opportunity, clearly from the advance of our knowledge even today, to catch up with a better understanding. However, that is certainly conditional. It cannot occur without the success of far future generations of humans, for which we must now account. In this time we are only on "the Edge of Forever".

Obviously, unless we everyday guard with every endeavor our precious children, to give their future children's-children the most humane chance, it is totally clear, that we will not mount Forever's elusive edge.

In the prequel to this book, "The Future Navigator" the following remains the relevant protecting container.

We are being day by day asked to develop a new kind of Mindfulness, one that leads to mental security for each person who is then progressing in a universal mindset as a member of the whole species. This will be an individual who recognizes that we can evolve, if we plan as one mentally expansive world community, we will see an awesome future.

It is why, the future protecting way, "The Vistavien Way" in these books is grounded on a special "Tactic of Behavior".

This is the philosophy of people that work to secure the progress of Human Kind into the future. It is an enlightened mindset yielding a sense of personal strength and promise!

The result is a protective blanket for children building future navigators who are armored mentally to create worldwide tolerance and peace.

Their way of thinking embraces human reason. This means first its caring ethics! Then it asks one to reject dogmatic pseudoscience and superstitions as the main basis of morality and decision making.

We may call this benevolent and wise philosophy "Objective Humanism". It is a continually adapting search for truth centered by a sense of humaneness. It holds intentionally that people be mentally free so that they can guard reasoning and subsequent actions!

Our ability to think, to be at first mindful and humane, is a gift so incredible, quite possibly, existing nowhere else in space and time that it would be the most terrible of all crimes ever-to lose that potential, through aberrations of greed and inhumanity.

It is a simple fact that we must---many more of us, see and feel it--our Vistavien Navigator self! Then and only then will there be earned for us....Heaven, Utopia, Shangri-La, Darul as-Salam for, for all time.

That is, of course, based upon sufficient time for us, the time to learn and grow, to practice our humanism!

If we achieve that, the story of human kind does not need to end untidy as it happens too frequently now. Then it could actually be as it may seem from distant outer space, one world, One-people!

GLOSSARY

Anthroposphere: The Anthroposphere (sometimes also referred as technosphere) is that part of the environment that is made or modified by humans for use in human activities and human habitats. It is one of the Earth's spheres.

Biogeochemistry: Biogeochemistry is the scientific discipline that involves the study of the chemical, physical, geological, and biological processes and reactions that govern the composition of the natural environment (including the biosphere, the cryosphere, the hydrosphere, the pedosphere, the atmosphere, and the lithosphere).

Collective Consciousness: Collective consciousness or collective conscious (French: conscience collective) is the set of shared beliefs, ideas and moral attitudes which operate as a unifying force within society. The term was introduced by the French sociologist Émile Durkheim in his Division of Labour in Society in 1893

Conscious Evolution: Conscious evolution refers to the claim that humanity has acquired the ability to choose what the species Homo sapiens becomes in the future, based on recent advancements in science, medicine, technology, psychology, sociology, and spirituality.

Global Brain: The global brain is a metaphor for the planetary ICT network that interconnects all humans and their technological artifacts.

<u>Hierchical-Task-Network</u>: In artificial intelligence, the hierarchical task network, or HTN, is an approach to automated planning in which the dependency among actions can be given in the form of networks. Planning problems are specified in the hierarchical task network approach by providing a set of tasks, which can be: primitive tasks, which roughly correspond to the actions of STRIPS; compound tasks, which can be seen as composed of a set of simpler tasks; goal tasks, which roughly corresponds to the goals of STRIPS, but are more general.

<u>Hypercyclic Morphogenesis</u>: Hypercyclic morphogenesis refers to the emergence of a higher order of self-reproducing structure or organization or hierarchy within a system. The hypercycle involves the problem in biochemistry of molecules combining in a self-reacting group that is able to stay together

<u>ICT</u>: Information and Communication Technology (ICT) is an extended term for information technology (IT) which stresses the role of unified communications and the integration of telecommunications (telephone lines and wireless signals), computers as well as necessary enterprise software, middleware, storage, and audio-visual.

<u>Ideosphere</u>: The Ideosphere, much like the Noosphere, is the realm of memetic evolution, just like the biosphere is the realm of biological evolution. It is the "place" where thoughts, theories and ideas are thought to be created, evaluated and evolved. The health of an Ideosphere can be measured by its memetic diversity. The Ideosphere is not considered to be a physical place by most people. It is instead

"inside the minds" of all the humans in the world. It is also, sometimes, believed that the Internet, books and other media could be considered to be part of the Ideosphere. Alas, as such media are not aware, it cannot process the thoughts it contains.

Infosphere: Coined by IBM, i.e. Infosphere Data Stage is an ETL tool and part of the IBM Information Platforms Solutions suite and IBM Infosphere. It uses a graphical notation to construct data integration solutions and is available in various versions such as the Server Edition, the Enterprise Edition, and the MVS Edition.

Knowledge Ecosystem: The idea of a knowledge ecosystem is an approach to knowledge management which claims to foster the dynamic evolution of knowledge interactions between entities to improve decision-making and innovation through improved evolutionary networks of collaboration.

Law of Complexity-Consciousness: The Law of Complexity-Consciousness (Complex Consciousness) is the postulated tendency of matter to become more complex over time and at the same time to become more conscious. The law was first formulated by Jesuit priest and paleontologist Pierre Teilhard de Chardin in his 1955 work "The Phenomenon of Man".

Memetics: Memetics is the theory of mental content based on an analogy with Darwinian evolution, originating from the popularization of Richard Dawkins' 1976 book "The Selfish Gene". Proponents describe Memetics as an approach to evolutionary models of cultural information transfer

<u>Noocracy</u>: Noocracy (/noʊˈɒkrəsi/ or /ˈnoʊ.əkrəsi/), or "aristocracy of the wise", as defined by Plato, is a social and political system that is "based on the priority of human mind", according to Vladimir Vernadsky.

<u>Noogenesis</u>: Noogenesis (Ancient Greek: νοῦς=mind + γένεσις = origin, becoming) is the emergence and evolution of intelligence.

<u>Noosphere</u>: A postulated sphere or stage of evolutionary development dominated by consciousness, the mind, and interpersonal relationships (frequently with reference to the writings of Teilhard de Chardin).

<u>Novel Ecosystem</u>: Novel ecosystems are human-built, modified, or engineered niches of the Anthropocene. They exist in places that have been altered in structure and function by human agency.

<u>Predictive Future</u>: That is, Predictive analytics encompasses a variety of statistical techniques from predictive modeling, machine learning, and data mining that analyze current and historical facts to make predictions about future or otherwise unknown events.

<u>Recapitulation Theory</u>: Recapitulation theory also called the biogenetic law or embryological parallelism is a biological hypothesis that the development of the embryo of an animal, from fertilization to gestation or hatching (ontogeny), goes through stages resembling or representing successive stages in the evolution of the animal's remote ancestors (phylogeny). Since embryos also evolve in different ways, the theory of

recapitulation is seen as a historical side-note, rather than as dogma in the field of developmental biology. Recapitulation theory has been applied and extended to several fields and areas, including the study of language (its origin), religion, biology, cognition and mental activities, anthropology, education theory and developmental psychology. Recapitulation theory is still considered plausible by some researchers in fields such as the study of the origin of language, cognitive development, and behavioral development in animals.

Theory of Intellect: a comprehensive theory about the nature and development of human intelligence. It was first created by the Swiss developmental psychologist Jean Piaget. The theory deals with the nature of knowledge itself and how humans gradually come to acquire, construct, and use it. Piaget's theory is mainly known as a developmental stage theory. In regards to the Global Brain, it is proposed that such as cyberspace activity can actuate various types of Global Thinking.

Universal Evolution: Universal evolution is a theory of evolution formulated by Pierre Teilhard de Chardin and Julian Huxley that describes the gradual development of the Universe from subatomic particles to human society, considered by Teilhard as the last stage.

Valtoos, Semandeks, and Noosfeer: Illustrations of the power and invasiveness of computer driven communication.
Valtoos are tools Included in the Actuarial Calculation Toolkit ACT (Actuarial Calculation Toolkit), is used by actuaries to define how a plan must be valued and how benefit

statements for that plan should be generated. ACT also allows the actuary to define how a plan's benefit estimation calculation is to be conducted, prior to final valuation. Semandeks are computer solutions for the most challenging data analysis tasks facing national security, law enforcement and information assurance professionals. Noosfeer is content for offline access on any device. Reduce mobile data usage when browsing the internet. You don't need an app to access offline!

Wayback Machine: The Wayback Machine is a digital archive of the World Wide Web and other information on the Internet created by the Internet Archive, a nonprofit organization, based in San Francisco, California, United States. The Internet Archive launched the Wayback Machine in October 2001. It was set up by Brewster Kahle and Bruce Gilliat, and is maintained with content from Alexa Internet. The service enables users to see archived versions of web pages across time, which the archive calls a "three dimensional index".

ACKNOWLEDGEMENTS

This book is composed around a series of proposals regarding thoughts related to the Noosphere and Omega, and a final result for human existence that are widely presented, discussed and even argued in popular discourse, and certainly in universities around the world. Indeed, as is frequently evident authors have debated as to who was first with this or that theory or title, (example Teilhard or Vernadsky or Le Roy, first using the term Noosphere). Consequently when appearing within this book the major thoughts are encapsulated into or under a series of subtitles which below are referenced multiply to pertinent sources for readers whilst the specific information contained has been edited and merged in the text as needed to present the dominant theme. For the reader who may wish to pursue these subjects even deeper they will find by entering Wikipedia, where reliability is specified, using the captions below vast citations and alternative views pertinent to the specific subjects.

Book Sub-Titles and Captions

Anthropocene (Anthroposphere)

Kuhn, A.; Heckelei, T., "Anthroposphere" pp 282-341, in "Impacts of Global Change on the Hydrological Cycle in West and Northwest Africa", ISBN: 978-3-642-12956-8 Springer Berlin Heidelberg, 2010

Artificial Intelligence

Crevier, Daniel (1993), AI: The Tumultuous Search for Artificial Intelligence, New York, NY: BasicBooks, ISBN 0-465-02997-3.

McCordick, Pamela (2004), Machines Who Think (2nd ed.), Natick, MA: A. K. Peters, Ltd., ISBN 1-56881-205-1.

THE OMEGA SHIELD

Newquist, HP (1994). The Brain Makers: Genius, Ego, and Greed in the Quest for Machines That Think. New York: Macmillan/SAMS. ISBN 0-672-30412-0.

Nilsson, Nils (2009). The Quest for Artificial Intelligence: History of Ideas and Achievements. New York: Cambridge University Press. ISBN 978-0-521-12293-1.

Biogeochemistry

Vladimir I. Vernadsky, 2007, Essays on Geochemistry & the Biosphere, tr. Olga Barash, Santa Fe, NM, Synergetic Press, ISBN 0-907791-36-0 (originally published in Russian in 1924).

Collective Consciousness:

Burns, T.R. Engdahl, E. (1998) the Social Construction of Consciousness. Part 1: Collective Consciousness and its Socio-Cultural Foundations, Journal of Consciousness Studies, 5 (1) p 77. Conscious Evolution

Kenneth Allan; Kenneth D. Allan (2 November 2005). Explorations in Classical Sociological Theory: Seeing the Social World. Pine Forge Press. P.108. ISBN 1-4129-0572-9

Evolution of Intelligence:

Eryomin A.L. The Laws of Evolution of the Mind, 7th International Teleconference on "Actual Problems of Modern Science". Tomsk, 2012. – P. 133-134.

Eryomin A.L. Noogenesis and Theory of Intellect. Krasnodar, 2005. — 356 p. (ISBN 5-7221-0671-2)

Global Brain:

Kelly, Kevin (1994). Out of control: The Rise of Neo-Biological Civilization. Reading, Mass: Addison-Wesley. pp. 5–28. ISBN 0201577933.

Mayer-Kress, G.; Barczys, C. (1995). "The global brain as an emergent structure from the Worldwide Computing Network, and its implications for modeling" this can be accessed in PDF form. The-Information-Society.11 (1):1–27.doi:10.1080/01972243.1995.9960177.

Heylighen, Francis (2011). "Conceptions of a Global Brain: an historical review" (PDF). In Grinin, L. E.; Carneiro, R. L.; Korotayev, A. V.; Spier, F. Evolution: Cosmic, Biological, and Social. Uchitel Publishing. pp. 274–289.

Helbing, Dirk (2015). "Creating ("Making") a Planetary Nervous System as Citizen Web". Thinking Ahead - Essays on Big Data, Digital Revolution, and Participatory Market Society. Springer International Publishing. pp. 189–194

Hierarchy of Needs:

Maslow, A.H. (1943). "A theory of human motivation". Psychological Review. 50 (4): 370–96 and "Farther Reaches of Human Nature", New York 1971, p. 269.

Mittelman, W. (1991). "Maslow's study of self-actualization: A reinterpretation". Journal of Humanistic Psychology. 31 (1): 114–135.

HTN-Hierarchical Task Network:

Erol, Kutluhan; Hendler, James; Nau, Dana S. (1996). "Complexity results for htn planning" (PDF). Annals of Mathematics and Artificial Intelligence. Springer. 18: 69–93. Retrieved 8 February 2015.

Alford, Ron; Bercher, Pascal; Aha, David (June 2015). Tight Bounds for HTN Planning (PDF). Proceedings of the 25th International Conference on Automated Planning and Scheduling (ICAPS). Retrieved 8 February 2015.

Alford, Ron; Kuter, Ugur; Nau, Dana S. (July 2009). Translating HTNs to PDDL: A small amount of domain knowledge can go a long way (PDF). Twenty-First International Joint Conference on Artificial Intelligence (IJCAI). Retrieved 8 February 2015

Hypercyclic Morphogenesis:

Alan M. Turing. "The Chemical Basis of Morphogenesis." Philosophical Transactions of the Royal Society B August 14, 1952, 237, pp. 37–72.

Manfred Eigen and Peter Schuster. The Hypercycle: A Principle of Natural Self-Organization. Berlin: Springer-Verlag, 1979

Ideosphere:

Best, M., L., 1997. Models for Interacting Populations of Memes: Competition and Niche Behavior. In the "Journal of Memetics Evolutionary Models of Information Transmission, 1. http://cfpm.org/jom-emit/1997/vol1/best_ml.html

Dawkins, R. 1976. "The Selfish Gene". Oxford: Oxford University Press.

Dennett, D. C. 1995. Darwin's Dangerous Idea. New York: Simon & Schuster.

Hofstadter, D. R. 1985. Metamagical Themas: Questing for the Essence of Mind and Pattern. New York: Basic Books.

Lynch, A. 1991. Thought Contagion as Abstract Evolution. Journal of Ideas, 2, 3-10. Republished with revisions at http://www.mcs.net/~aaron/mememath.html. Scanned at http://www.mcs.net/~aaron/Lynch1991.htm.

Infosphere:

McBurney, Vincent (2006), "Lee Scheffler Interview - the Ghost of Data Stage present", Tooling Around in the IBM Infosphere (Search directly IBM their Infosphere).

Knowledge Ecosystem:

Choo,C.,Bontis,Nick (2002). The Strategic Management of Intellectual Capital and Organizational Knowledge. New York: Oxford University Press. ISBN 0-19-515486-X

Consciousness:

Geraldine O. Browning; Joseph L. Alioto; Seymour M. Farber (1973). Teilhard de Chardin: in Quest of the Perfection of Man: An International Symposium. Fairleigh Dickinson Univ. Press. p. 127.

Memetics:

Boyd, Robert & Richardson, Peter J. (1985). Culture and the Evolutionary Process. Chicago University Press. ISBN 978-0-226-06933-3

Boyd, Rob & Richardson, Peter J. (2005). Not by Genes Alone: How Culture Transformed Human Evolution. Chicago University Press. ISBN 0-226-71284-2

Edmonds, Bruce. 2005. "The revealed poverty of the gene-meme analogy – why Memetics per se has failed." Journal of Memetics - Evolutionary Models of Information Transmission, 9

Aunger, Robert. The Electric Meme: A New Theory of How We Think. New York: Free Press, 2002. ISBN 978-0-7432-0150-6

The Meme Machine by Susan Blackmore, Oxford University Press, 1999, hardcover ISBN 0-19-850365-2, trade paperback ISBN 0-9658817-8-4, May 2000, ISBN 0-19-286212-X

Noocracy:

Art & Scientific Research Are Free, European Commission, European Commission Community research, Semar Publishers Srl, 2005, ISBN 88-7778-102-5, ISBN 978-88-7778-102-4

Noogenesis:

Pierre Teilhard de Chardin The Phenomenon of Man. Harper Torchbooks, The Cloister Library, Harper & Row, Publishers, 1961, p. 273.

Steinhart E. Teilhard de Chardin and Transhumanism // Journal of Evolution and Technology — Vol. 20 Issue 1 - December 2008 — pgs. 1-22 ISSN 1541-0099

Eryomin A.L. Noogenesis and Theory of Intellect. Krasnodar, 2005. — p.20, p.331.

Noosphere:

Norgaard, R. B. (1994). Development betrayed: the end of progress and a coevolutionary revisioning of the future. London; New York, Routledge. ISBN 0-415-06862-2

Samson, Paul R.; Pitt, David (eds.) (1999), the Biosphere and Noosphere Reader: Global Environment, Society and Change. ISBN 0-415-16644-6

Georgy S. Levit: "The Biosphere and the Noosphere Theories of V. I. Vernadsky and P. Teilhard de Chardin: A Methodological Essay. International Archives on the History of Science/Archives Internationales D'Histoire des Sciences", 50 (144), 2000: p. 160–176

Novel Ecosystems:

Williams, R.; Sörensen, K. H., eds. (2002). "The cultural shaping of technologies and the politics of technodiversity." Shaping Technology, Guiding Policy: Concepts, Spaces & Tools. Cheltenham: Edward Elgar. pp. 173–194. ISBN 1-84064-649-7.

Monserie, M.; Watteau, F.; Villemin, G.; Ouvrard, S.; Morel, J. (2009). "Technosol genesis: identification of organo-mineral associations in a young Technosol derived from coking plant waste materials". J Soils Sediments. 9: 537–546.

Theory of Intellect:

Mamedova M.D. The Concept of "Mind" in Chinese and Russian Linguistic Morld-images (on the material of phraseological units, proverbs and sayings). Dushanbe: Russian-Tajik (Slavonic) University, 2015. 245 pp.

Universal Evolution:

Paul R. Samson and David Pitt (eds.) (1999), the Biosphere and Noosphere Reader: Global Environment, Society and Change. ISBN 0-415-16644-6

"The Quest for the Unified Theory of Information" [permanent dead link], World Futures, Volumes 49 (3-4) & 50 (1-4) 1997, Special Issue

Norgaard, R. B. (1994). Development betrayed: the end of progress and a coevolutionary revisioning of the future. London; New York, Routledge. ISBN 0-415-06862-2

~~~~~~

A sincere apology is offered if an originating author has been missed when the technical thoughts are presented.

If you are in that category, please address your concern to the Author at Minds-Eye @bresnan.net. Corrections will then be posted on the Manuscript's Web Site www.aminds-eyejourney.net.

All the persons in the Forever Panel are representative of those with whom the Author is acquainted, names are changed to protect privacy.

The author is sincerely grateful for the critical review of the manuscript conducted by Dr. Elisabet Nalvarte, and for the text editing by Carol McGraw.

THE AUTHOR

D.M. Yourtee, is Professor Emeritus, University of Missouri, USA where he was many years a teacher in the Schools of Pharmacy, Medicine and Dentistry. His medical research and scholarly record are well recorded in the scientific literature. Recognitions include Marquis Who's Who in Science and Engineering, and America's Registry of Outstanding Professionals.

This writing was created through his experience when he was a Senior Fulbright Scholar and Researcher Africa-Area-Wide "and his subsequent world journeys related to that humanitarian research.

Dr.Yourtee's books originate as "Minds-Eye Manuscripts"™, writings which take positions on past and probable future history. At time of this publication those manuscripts have been made into soft cover volumes that can be obtained at http://www.aminds-eyejourney.net. All the works are created to remind us about tolerance on behalf of our children and the potential of human kind.

He notes that his books do not always treat kindly the actions of the various faiths in what he calls their 'Spirit Wars"the too often inhumanity, though as these books develop they show the beginning benevolent foundations in all the faiths, and ways for folks to look clearly toward options for their children, eyeing their eventual adulthood in our conflicted world.

In retirement Dr. Yourtee resides in Grand Junction Colorado where he enjoys watching his grand-children grow up and addressing he hopes, through writing his books-useful ideas for securing their health and happiness and that same for all the forthcoming generations.

Should the reader wish to communicate with the author your comments would be gratefully received through web mail address futurespeak@bresnan.net.

Fortifying the Omega Shield

Thankfully, humans do have a benevolent predisposition that will preserve them---if it is not lost through too many corrupting influences worming into their developing Global Brain!

Of course, censorship is not the answer. However, untoward effects will likely happen through mind warping powers implanted in cyberspace. People who care[1] will, consequently, need records of troublesome cyberspace threats. That is, evidence of those "insidious insertions" prompting people to adapt in ways their benevolent predisposition otherwise would not choose to go! A few examples follow and more should be added, upon readers consideration. The below were published in 2017, various news media making us aware. More of these may also be found in the book.

Memes and Facebook. This report is extracted from "The Morning Briefing Paper". "It's all fun and games until someone's password security question gets hacked. Here is an example. A meme making the rounds on Facebook asks users to list 10 concerts -nine they've attended and a fabricated one. It then invites others to identify the fake one. But the post "10 Concerts I've been To, One is a Lie" might also be an invitation to a midlevel threat to your online privacy and security, experts said. The meme, which surged in popularity this week, is the kind of frivolous distraction that makes up social media interactions, similar to other viral memes, such as the "Ice Bucket Challenge".(Remember how so many people adopted their behavior for this.)

However, privacy experts cautioned it could reveal too much about a person's background and preferences and sounds like a

---

1.See page 111 for amplification on the "Skies" Proposal. This argues for world-wide cyberspace analytical groups to be organized as a formal part of the Omega Shield.

security question- name the first concert you attended -that you might be asked on a banking, brokerage or similar website to verify your identity. Michael Kaiser, the executive director of the "National Cyber Security Alliance", said "that the meme posed a moderate security risk, adding that not every website relied on a security question about a person's first concert. He said, further that the greater danger is what such a list might broadly reveal through social engineering. It could telegraph information about a user's age, musical tastes and even religious affiliation, all of which would be desirable to marketers hoping to target ads." (and so influence the susceptible).

He said "it is similar to users who take quizzes on Facebook. The answers can reveal specifics about a person's upbringing, culture or other identifying details. You are expressing things about you, maybe in more subtle ways than you might think," he said. Mark Testoni, a national security and privacy expert who is chief executive of SAP National Security Services, said in an email "that he recommended exercising "vigilance bordering on a little paranoia" in online posts. We need to understand how we interact can disclose not only specific details but patterns of behavior and often our location, among other things," he wrote.

"Companies, governments and other groups rely on so-called authenticators, such as "What is your mother's maiden name?" Such answers are not truly authenticators, but are facts." "The usual aphorism is: 'Your password should be secret, but 'secrets' make really bad passwords' especially when they are just discoverable or guessable facts" Mr. Kaiser agreed. "In cases where the answer to a security question is easily obtained such as what high school did you attend? ---It's best to make up an answer, even if it's not as easy to recall. His advice about online quizzes and memes was not meant to be a killjoy, though he encouraged social media users to consider the consequences of what they share. People always have to have their eyes wide open when they're on the internet," he said. "It's the way of the world!" That is already of this time. It can be seen, the need for vigilance, gathering a person's persona allows development of means to stimulate it in ways undesirable, but not easily foreseen.

Artificial Intelligence Influences: This report is drawn from Microsoft's "Annual Build Conference". Microsoft on Wednesday unveiled new tools intended to "Democratize artificial intelligence (AI) by enabling machine smarts to be built into software from smartphone games to factory floors." The US technology titan opened its annual Build Conference by highlighting programs with artificial intelligence that could tap into services in the internet "cloud" and even take advantage of computing power in nearby machines.

"We are infusing AI into every product and service we offer," said Microsoft executive vice president of artificial intelligence and research Harry Shum. "We've been creating the building blocks for the current wave of AI breakthroughs for more than two decades." Microsoft research has gone deep into areas such as machine learning, speech recognition, and enabling machines to recognize what they "see." "Now, we're in the unique position of being able to use those decades of research breakthroughs," Shum said. Microsoft rivals including Amazon, Apple, Google and IBM have all been aggressively pursuing the promise and potential of artificial intelligence as well. Artificial intelligence is getting a foothold in people's homes, with personal assistants answering questions and controlling connected devices such as appliances or light bulbs. Digital assistants already boast features such as reminding people of appointments entered into calendars and chiming in with advice to set out early if traffic is challenging."

However, and this is critical input, to which there must be overt attention! Microsoft chief executive Satya Nadella, who opened the Seattle conference, also highlighted the need to build trust in technology, saying "new applications must avoid the dystopian futures feared by some. Nadella's presentation included images from George Orwell's "1984" and Aldous Huxley's "Brave New World" to underscore the issue of responsibility of those creating new technologies."

"What Orwell prophesied in '1984,' where technology was being used to monitor, control, dictate, or what Huxley imagined we may do just by distracting ourselves without any meaning or purpose," Nadella said. "Neither of these futures is something that we want... The future of computing is going to be defined by the choices that you as developers make and the impact of those choices on the world." (Is it not clear, that while the "desire" to not have an Orwell prophesy a reality, there are not also formulated preventative means, rules or codes?)

The Bloggers: The Silicon Valley entrepreneur Williams first drew notice during the dot-com boom, for developing software that allowed users to easily set up a website for broadcasting their thoughts: blogging. By the time Google bought the company in 2003, more than a million people were using it. Then came Twitter, which wasn't his idea but was his company. Then begins the posting the events "of concern for all to tell us". The owner recently commented about his consequent cyberlink invention. "A few years ago, Twitter was viewed as a tool of liberation. It enabled, some believed, the Arab Spring uprisings in the Middle East. Twitter, like the internet itself, was putting tyranny on a short leash. Then the narrative turned darker, with the rise of trolling on the platform. People are using Facebook to showcase suicides, beatings and murder, in real time. And, Twitter is a hive of trolling and abuse that it seems unable to stop. Fake news, whether created for ideology or profit, runs rampant. Four out of 10 adult internet users said in a Pew survey that they had been harassed online. And that was before the presidential campaign heated providing a new avenue for lies and innuendo. I thought once everybody could speak freely and exchange information and ideas, the world is automatically going to be a better place," Mr. Williams says. "I was wrong about that." He and others are currently hoping to correct such software programing to avoid the pitfalls. (But it is out there and influencing thought already! Lesson learned?)

The Brain Computer Interface: As noted on page 78 there are "Silicon Expert Companies" backing brain implant-computer interface ventures (one is called "Neuralink" another "Kernel'). As various articles tell this is ongoing and here is updated, one of many needed as vigilance is required in shielding of Human Evolution toward Omega.

What Neuralink and new Kernel are trying to do is take the first steps toward hacking the brain, so to speak, so that human beings can in the future stay healthier for longer and potentially enjoy the benefits of treating the human brain like a computing platform. This means using a chip inside the skull or some other electronic device that could improve our memory and our ability to perform complex mental tasks, as well as increase speed at which we could communicate with one another. It could even allow us to directly link with the internet cloud and other forms of internet infrastructure. (This sounds impossible, and right now it may be)

The entrepreneurs involved think that improving human cognition is the surest path forward for humanity. To quote one of them, "I think if humanity were to identify a singular thing to work on, the thing that would demand the greatest minds of our generation, it's human intelligence," (This, however, seems at present to avoid recognizing that it is current homo sapiens who have traveled to the moon, created skyscrapers and antibiotics, then kill each other in wars with little sensible justification. Is it not more important that humans improve their sense of humanity, and that of course can only come with patience in living actual life and worldwide tolerance education?) The good side of these star wars ideas is, of course, that they may funnel greater funding into neurological medical research.

Currently, the arguments are pro and con as to the actual in practice use of this cyber technology. A severely paralyzed man with such an implant may be able to eat and drink. On the other hand while most healthy individuals are uncomfortable with the idea of having a doctor crack open their skull a good many people use mind expanding drugs such as marijuana (weed), that is the drive for satisfaction, thrill and ease of the days challenges is, of course, universal. " Obviously, people implanted (Neurolinked) are fully susceptible to most any suggestion, through "their" cyber neurons!

'The Default Effect[1]: Software and entertainment companies exploit the tendency to empower programs to collect as much data as possible from consumers, or to keep us glued to our seats for "one more episode" of a streaming show.'

Even so and critical to realizing the reality of cyberspace control, overall---"the fact is only five percent of users ever change these settings, despite widespread concerns about how companies might be using collected information or manipulating people's choices and thoughts! And, it is noted, even when people are unhappy with a state of affairs, they are usually disinclined to change it. This is documented in the cognitive and behavioral sciences and is known as the "default effect."

So in the face of this, the future navigator would say...How do good intentions hold when control is within an ever expanding Global Brain, running worldwide amuck?

It is, bluntly, a matter of vigilance, attention to intention! Concern and alertness returned to the Global Brain, is a counter measure - a means of clearing the "Brains Mind".

Not defaulting? Continue this list! Watch influences and resulting behavior in those new ones, the new generations coming into the age of the Global Brain! Stand against it degrading your humanity!

''

1.Huh, Young Eun; Vosgerau, Joachim; Morewedge, Carey K. (2014-10-01). "Social Defaults: Observed Choices Become Choice Defaults". Journal of Consumer Research

CPSIA information can be obtained
at www.ICGtesting.com
Printed in the USA
BVHW040558171221
624022BV00025B/1476

9 781006 269332